A
CLASSICAL RIDING
NOTEBOOK

A
CLASSICAL RIDING
NOTEBOOK
Michael J. Stevens

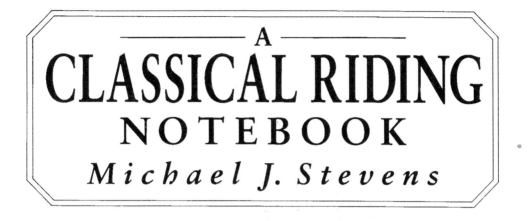
KENILWORTH PRESS

First published in 1994 by
The Kenilworth Press Ltd
Addington
Buckingham
MK18 2JR

British Library Cataloguing in Publication Data
A catalogue record for this book is available from the British Library.

ISBN 1 872082- 50-5

Text design: Paul Saunders
Line drawings: Dianne Breeze
Layout and typesetting: Kenilworth Press Ltd
Printed and bound by
Hillman Printers (Frome) Ltd

Contents

Foreword by Charles de Kunffy   9
Preface   11
Acknowledgements   12
Introduction   13

1. THE ESSENTIALS OF RIDING   17
Equitation
   The Seat / The Legs / The Arms / Moving with the Horse
The Principles of Control

2. THE ESSENTIALS OF TRAINING   27
Active Forward Movement
   The Requirement / Rider Interference / The Lazy Horse /
   Physiological Problems
Putting the Horse on the Aids
   Horse Behind the Bit / Horse Above the Bit / How NOT to
     put the Horse on the Aids
Straightening the Horse
   Causes of Crookedness / Signs of Crookedness / Summary of
     Requirements / Techniques for Straightening the Horse

3. BALANCE   51
Testing for Balance
Techniques for Improving Balance

4. RESISTANCES 56
Common Causes of Resistance

5. PROGRESSIVE LATERAL WORK 59
Early Beginnings
The Turn on the Forehand / The Leg-Yield
Useful Gymnastic Exercises
The Shoulder-in / The Haunches-in and the Half-Pass /
The Full Pass
Advanced Lateral Movements
The Passade / The Pirouette

6. AIDS FOR BENDING AND LATERAL MOVEMENTS 71
Bending
Lateral Exercises
Shoulder-in / Haunches-in / Half-Pass

7. FLYING CHANGES 79
Teaching the Flying Change
Teaching Multiple Flying Changes

8. EXTREMES OF COLLECTION 85
Teaching the Piaffe and the Passage
The Piaffe / The Passage
Teaching the Canter Pirouette

9. TRAINING PROCEDURE 99
Early Preparations
Lungeing
Initial Ridden Training
Schooling in the Second Year
Schooling in the Third Year
Schooling in the Fourth and Subsequent Years

10. REMEDIAL SCHOOLING 111

11. HELPFUL HINTS AND REMINDERS   115

INFLUENTIAL RIDING MASTERS   120

Bibliography   124
Index   127

Foreword

by Charles de Kunffy

Dressage is the systematic, gradual and knowledgeable development of the horse's inherent athletic potential. Dressage riding, and the training of horses based on its principles, depends on scholarly observation, academic preparedness and loyalty to the body of classical equestrian knowledge. Dressage is not an isolated discipline, but rather it is scientific riding and training based on principles that succeed with most horses most of the time. It is relevant to all riders interested in horsemanship for the sake of the horse.

Today's riders enjoy a great advantage over riders of past centuries in that equestrian literature is easily accessible. There can never be too many good books on the subject of classical horsemanship.

Horses need not be fancy to develop athletically and give great satisfaction to their riders. Ordinary horses, like the common 'remounts' of the past, are deserving of our love and respect and should be beneficiaries of our equestrian expertise. Dressage riding is no longer a privilege of the wealthy or members of the military. Average people with average economic means can now pursue classical horsemanship. People are drawn to this sport, recognising its great rewards in offering participation in art while remaining intimately in touch with nature. The longing for things natural, for the companionship of a beautiful creature, serve well the needs of urbanised people overwhelmed by a mechanised and quantified world. People are starved of humanising endeavours that enrich the spirit, mature the emotions, inspire the imagination, and cultivate the mind, and the horse presents itself as the modern man's consolation prize.

Dressage is nothing new; its ways are not innovative and its mastery is not quick and easy. The art of dressage remains defiantly and graciously un-modern. Its fundamentals, the classical principles of equitation and of schooling horses, are centuries old and depend on our dedicated scholarship for learning them.

Michael Stevens, the author of this volume, remains loyal to the principles of classical horsemanship. Practising the tradition's cherished value for humility, the author offers no revolutionary break-throughs or stunning insights. Instead, he presents us with a collection of the most important riding principles that remain a part of established classical equestrian wisdom. The author shares his scholarship, his thoughts and his insights with like-minded people and squanders no energy on arguing in defence of the obvious values.

In this fine volume, Michael Stevens helps his readers to become aware of the reasons why we ride the way we do. He succeeds in conveying the meaning, usefulness and appropriateness of the various gymnastic exercises. He does a great service in making the reader aware that riding is rational and that the work with the horse is systematic. He puts great emphasis on riding correctly and doing useful exercises to benefit horses.

The author offers an unpretentious advocacy of the traditional equitational principles. He does it in a succinct style, phrased clearly in language that is easy to comprehend, and his material is logically organised. These are valuable assets in learning the contents of his work. He addresses the principles of horsemanship with constant emphasis on the love of, and appreciation for, the horse.

A welcome addition to the body of classical equestrian literature.

Charles de Kunffy
Pacifica, California

Preface

This book has evolved over a period of several years from notes I made while learning the principles and practice of schooling horses according to the classical tradition. Originally I wrote the notes in order to clarify my own understanding of the subject, but I believe they might also form a useful guide for others who are seeking information on how to ride and train horses.

Although I have derived the information from personal experience in the saddle, this has been influenced by watching some of the world's top trainers, and by making extensive studies of equestrian literature. Consequently the book represents an explanation of existing methods; I am not introducing any new concepts. I have attended most of the regular visits to England of the author and international coach Charles de Kunffy. Mr de Kunffy's teaching methods and his lectures, which are always delivered with unparalleled clarity, have had a major impact on my thinking, and have shown me new horizons.

Many books on riding are heavy going, and it is often difficult to find all the pertinent information in one volume. Here I have tried to assemble the most important ideas into a concise, readable form. I hope that it will assist in the comprehension of the fundamentals, and help to foster an interest in classical riding.

Acknowledgements

I would like to thank everyone who has been involved in the production of this book.

Lesley Gowers, Managing Editor, who directed the publication, also offered knowledgeable advice on the material to be included, and obtained the photographs. I much appreciate all her hard work and her generous patronage of a new author.

Dianne Breeze has put a great deal of effort into producing the superb illustrations. They complement the text far better than I could have imagined and I cannot thank her enough.

I could not be more pleased that Charles de Kunffy was willing to write the Foreword. It is an honour indeed to be able to include some paragraphs from a recognised master and ambassador of classical riding, and I am most grateful.

Michael J Stevens
25th January 1994

Introduction

O ver a period of several centuries a scientific and systematic
method of training the riding horse has evolved, and because
of its merits it has come to be known as classical riding. The alternatives are either ad hoc or forceful, and the results cannot match
those that can be obtained by the classical system. The method is
applicable to all riding horses regardless of whether they are to be
used as eventers, show jumpers, hacks or dressage horses. It can be
used by all riders who wish to develop the potential of their horses
so as to render them more versatile mounts and a greater pleasure
to ride.

First and foremost it is necessary for the rider to develop the right
attitude to the horse. He must understand a little of equine psychology
and be able to understand the horse's behaviour and language.
Through his knowledge of the species and his imagination he should
have some idea of what it must be like to be a horse, and how the horse
thinks and feels.

The rider must have an interest in getting to the root of a problem and
have the ability to solve it without resorting to unnecessary force. The
rider who resorts to strong bits or other gadgets has little hope of
success and will not bring his horses to their full potential. A talented
horseman can get good results out of any horse, whereas an inexperienced rider who cannot be troubled to learn may be able to get

satisfactory results only from expensive animals that do not need so much help. There are no short cuts in training horses, but with experience the task gets easier and all horses seem to have more potential than was previously imagined.

Provided classical principles are applied from the start of their training most horses are capable of reaching medium dressage level; it is only for advanced work that a horse with special talents is needed. Sadly only a small proportion of horses in Britain ever reach medium level. This is partly because their early schooling is often done badly so they lack a proper foundation, partly because riders lack the knowledge or the inclination to school their horses beyond the most basic levels, and partly because the riding profession lacks the necessary expertise.

The profession in Britain has no traditional background in dressage, and although the situation is improving, in practical terms the training of the horse is still not considered a major priority. Most horses used in riding schools receive next to no schooling. This makes it very difficult for students to be able to distinguish right from wrong and to appreciate how wonderful it can be to ride a horse that has received a thorough education.

When a rider buys a horse of his own after completing a course of instruction at a riding school it is most unlikely that he will have been taught a schooling method. It is also unlikely that his horse will have received anything but a very basic education. Often the rider will run out of ideas after a few minutes schooling, and will then give up and go out for a hack instead. Those who wish to succeed in dressage competitions can avoid making a thorough study of training by buying a well-schooled horse and by seeking the help of an experienced trainer. Under the circumstances it is very difficult for the art of riding to flourish.

Schooling the horse is an activity in which every horse owner should become involved. Really it is not very difficult, and it is certainly very rewarding. An expert would expect to be able to break in and train a horse up to Grand Prix level in the space of some three or four years.

Although it may take a year or two longer, these higher levels can be reached by any enthusiastic dedicated rider, amateur or professional, so long as the basic principles are understood and the training is built on a sound foundation.

CHAPTER ONE

The Essentials of Riding

Equitation for schooling on the flat is more critical than many other branches of riding because of the fine degree of control required. It is worthwhile putting a lot of effort into perfecting the correct position and motion in the saddle because everything in riding depends on how well these are mastered. If the position departs from the ideal then the aids will become less effective, and some of the rider's interactions with his horse will be counter-productive. If the rider cannot move in harmony with his horse then the latter will be unable to move with freedom or grace.

There are many possible ways in which the rider can influence the horse, but there are good ways and bad ways; some can be detrimental to the horse's training. In everyday life man uses his hands a great deal, but in fact they are not very useful for controlling the horse. On horseback the rider must overcome this natural desire to use the hands for everything, and must learn to apply a proper system of control.

Riding involves a two-way communication between horse and rider, and the latter must also be receptive to the signals that he receives from his companion. He must be able to assess continually the quality of all those factors that comprise the horse's performance, and take corrective action before a problem develops to the stage where it is difficult to handle. He must also be sensitive enough to feel all the horse's imperfections so that he can plan the schooling accordingly by selecting remedial exercises calculated to strengthen the particular weaknesses shown by the horse.

Equitation

The Seat

Opinions are divided on exactly how the seat of the rider should contact the saddle. Traditionally the classical seat has a three-point contact, comprising the two seat bones and the crotch. A slight natural hollow in the small of the back enables the body to balance in a static equilibrium, and allows the rider to give very subtle weight aids. The rider should be careful not to hollow his back deliberately or he will lose all his effectiveness. In fact the feeling should be more one of trying to straighten the lower back; but under normal circumstances it need not be flattened completely. The rider should ensure that no part of his weight is supported by the thighs or by the stirrups, as then he would no longer have a three-point seat.

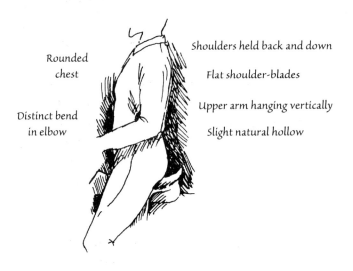

Rounded chest

Distinct bend in elbow

Shoulders held back and down

Flat shoulder-blades

Upper arm hanging vertically

Slight natural hollow

Correct positioning of the rider's upper body.

This side view of Arthur Kottas-Heldenberg, Chief Rider of the Spanish Riding School of Vienna, shows how the rider's position should be upright yet relaxed. Notice that his heels lie directly beneath his seat, and that his upper body appears to be slightly behind the vertical. The obvious lack of tension in the reins demonstrates the correctness of the contact with the bit. *(Photo: Michael Stevens)*

The upper body should be balanced above the area where the seat contacts the saddle. No muscular effort is required for a balanced seat, except that there must be sufficient muscle tone in the torso to prevent it from collapsing. When properly balanced the torso will appear to be slightly behind the vertical. This is illustrated in many old equestrian portraits, and it is also demonstrated by modern Grand Prix dressage riders.

The upper body should not lean in front of the vertical, or the rider would have to exert some muscular effort to prevent it falling forwards. The horse would then have difficulty in bringing his hind legs far enough forward to carry the weight; he would be inclined to get 'on the forehand'. If problems arise which necessitate stronger aiding, the rider may have to flatten his back, and he might even have to lean behind the vertical. This is not the same as being behind the movement, which occurs when the rider is surprised by a sudden forward spring from the horse, momentarily loses his balance and tips backwards.

The shoulders must be held back and down, with the shoulder-blades flat against the back. Viewed from the side the shoulders should be at the back of the torso, with a rounded chest in front. It is very difficult to use the back correctly if the shoulders are rounded. If they were rounded then the rider would have to lean further back to achieve a balanced position, and this would adversely affect the horse's paces.

The Legs

The rider's legs should hang down naturally under their own weight so that the heels are positioned below the seat. The feet should be turned so that the toes point towards the front and the inside of the calves rest gently against the horse's sides. Each stirrup should carry no more than the weight of the foot hanging from a loose ankle. The feet should be placed against the outside edges of the stirrup irons, and the toes should project an inch or two beyond the irons so that the point of contact lies just in front of the ball of the foot. The main purpose of the stirrups is to prevent the legs from hanging down so far that they splay out away from the horse's sides. The rider should not depend on the stirrups or allow them to affect his horsemanship. He must ride in the same way that he would if they were taken away.

The rider should never use his legs in a backwards direction, and the knee joint should not close when the legs are applied, or the seat will lighten and the aids will be less effective. The legs should be applied in a slightly forwards direction against the lay of the horse's coat. This enables the rider to increase the effectiveness of his seat at the same time.

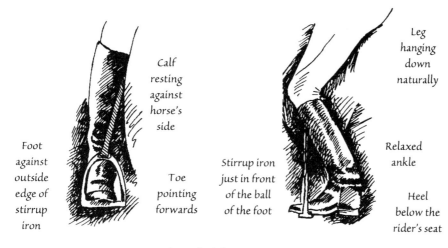

The rider's leg position.

Labels on the illustration:

- Calf resting against horse's side
- Leg hanging down naturally
- Foot against outside edge of stirrup iron
- Toe pointing forwards
- Stirrup iron just in front of the ball of the foot
- Relaxed ankle
- Heel below the rider's seat

The Arms

The rider's upper arm must hang down vertically so that the elbows lie close to the hips. There must be a well-defined bend at the elbows. The hands should be held low down, just above the horse's withers, with the wrists straight and the thumbs uppermost. The hands should be close together so that the knuckles are almost touching.

The horse must feel that the reins are connected to the rider's seat. The feeling must be very similar to having side-reins attached. A common fault is to give the horse the feeling that the reins are connected to dangling arms which can be dislodged at will by any movement of the head and neck.

Commonly the rider is taught to take up the reins until he makes contact with the horse's mouth, and then told to follow all the movements made by the horse in order to keep the pressure on the reins constant. This 'non-interference' doctrine owes nothing to the classical school; historically it came about because of changing attitudes in society. People were no longer prepared to put their horses through time-consuming schooling programmes, and furthermore they wanted to ride without the trouble of learning the subtleties of

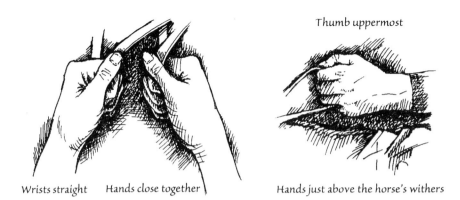

Thumb uppermost

Wrists straight   Hands close together   Hands just above the horse's withers

Holding the reins.

equitation. In the context of 'the uneducated' riding 'the unschooled' this non-interference policy is less harmful to the horse, but it is not a strategy to be adopted by those seeking to improve their horses. The rider should harmonise the movements of his body with those of the horse when the latter moves correctly, but he must not allow the horse to move in any way he likes or he will avoid his work, and remain green for the rest of his life.

If the horse moves at walk or canter with massive oscillations of his head and neck then he is not carrying himself properly, and the rider should never piston backwards and forwards with his hands to accommodate such faulty locomotion. Instead the rider must take positive action to get the horse on the aids. When the horse is moving properly through his back then the bit will be the termination point for his energies and his head and neck will remain still.

The rider's task is to present the bit as a moving barrier. When the horse is driven towards it he will engage his hind legs, arch his back, and flex his poll. The rider who yields the reins to follow all the horse's actions removes the barrier altogether, and so has no means of improving the horse's balance. The reins should be yielded slightly as a reward for moving correctly, and to encourage further relaxation and stretching. The rider should alternate the yielding so that it only occurs on one side at a time: it should be co-ordinated with the forward progression of the horse's shoulder on the same side, since it will then encourage the development of free paces.

The tension in the reins should be kept to an absolute minimum, and should never be allowed to interfere with the horse's natural head carriage. There should never be a backward pull on the reins. The rider should imagine that the reins are made of thread; the tension should never be sufficient to break the thread. Riding the horse in greater collection must also involve a lightening of the contact. Collection cannot be achieved by shortening the horse's neck. The horse should be kept in self-carriage so he is not supporting himself on the bit.

If there is a problem with the horse's head carriage then this is often a symptom of a problem in the horse's back or hindquarters. Problems in riding cannot be solved by working on the symptoms, and any inter- ference via the reins will only lead to more discomfort for the horse.

Moving with the Horse

believer in
doing sitting
trot

Before attempting to school a horse the rider should master the sitting trot. To discover what the ideal sitting trot feels like the rider should put his horse into a trot, hold the saddle arch and pull himself down into the saddle. The horse would certainly suffer from an actual bumping on his back, but ideally he should not even have to contend with a pressure variation. The rider should be able to hold his legs out sideways away from the horse so that the seat is the only contact point, and still do a good sitting trot for a few strides.

The rider must allow his lower back to move in such a way that he can conform to the movement in the horse's back without suffering any jarring. The upper body should give the appearance of stillness. Some riders can be seen swaying backwards and forwards, and others nod their heads continually as the horse moves. Such riders are absorbing the movement further up the vertebral column and are not moving their lumbar region sufficiently.

The walk and trot are symmetrical paces: both sides of the horse's body move one after the other in an identical way. Consequently the motion of the rider's lower back will feel the same on both sides. At canter, however, the horse leads with either the left or the right, and the two sides of his body move differently. The movement of horse and rider at a left lead canter will be the mirror image of the movement at a right lead canter. In order to conform to the motion at canter the rider must gyrate his pelvis but keep his upper body still; it should not sway backwards and forwards. There should be a feeling of pushing the inside seat bone down and forwards at each stride. When necessary the rider can increase the driving power by gyrating his upper body and hips together so that the push comes from the forward movement of his inside shoulder.

The Principles of Control

The horse is controlled by actions of the rider's body, legs and hands, which engage in a continual dialogue with the horse and form an **aiding system**. As the name suggests, the **aids** should assist the horse to produce the required response. This should come about by means of a combination of natural reactions and learned responses, conducted in a spirit of co-operation.

The rider should aim to control the horse mostly through his own pelvis. Ninety per cent of aiding should be through judicious use of stomach, back and thigh muscles which affect the motion of the pelvis and control the horse by encouraging or damping down the motion in his back. There is a popular but misguided view that pressure on the horse's mouth forms part of the braking mechanism. In fact it cannot compel the horse to stop because it does nothing to prevent him using his legs. Furthermore, the horse cannot escape the pressure by slowing down or stopping, on account of the fact that he carries his rider with him. Consequently stopping is not a natural response to pressure on the mouth. The horse will only slow down if he remembers from experience that the rider will lighten the contact when he does so.

Often the rider will resort to a stronger bit to gain the extra mechanical advantage. Although it can sometimes be easier to get a transition in

Control of the horse should always appear effortless, as shown in this picture of Isabell Werth on Gigolo in extended trot. The horse's motion does not disturb the rider's seat, and the rider does nothing to impede the horse's locomotion. *(Photo: Werner Ernst)*

this way, the quality will suffer. Gradually the horse's hind legs will engage to a lesser extent, his balance will consequently deteriorate and this will render him even harder to stop.

If the horse is properly trained and ridden, then the rider should scarcely need to use the reins. Ancient writings have been discovered which describe how, in the second century BC, war horses were ridden without bridles. The riders controlled their mounts by means of a rope attached to a halter, and a cane. Today in Spain and Portugal there are stages in bull-fighting when the toreadors drop the reins and yet remain in perfect control in very dangerous situations.

The only satisfactory way to encourage the horse to stop is for the rider to slow down the rhythmic movement of his pelvis which will thereby damp down the movement in the horse's back. The rider can achieve this by closing his knees and thighs more firmly against the saddle, and by tightening his stomach muscles. The rider who believes otherwise, or who cannot trouble himself to learn to stop by using his seat rather than the reins, will certainly fail in his attempts at schooling the horse. Mastery of this technique is one of the keys to success in riding and training horses. To achieve a good quality transition the rider may need to use legs and hands to keep the hind legs engaged and to prevent the horse from poking his nose, but the dominant stopping aid must always be given to the horse through the rider's seat. If the horse will not stop it is better for his development to ride him straight up to a wall than to pull on the reins.

Closely related to the halt is a movement known as the **half-halt**. This can be used for improving the horse's balance and checking his speed. It should be performed in exactly the same way as a downward transition, the only difference being that when the rider feels that the horse is about to perform the transition he relaxes the aids and allows him to continue in the original pace in self-carriage. The point is that in order to re-balance the horse it is not necessary to perform the complete transition. This relaxation of the aids is the key to producing lightness in the horse. The ideal half-halt is brought about by the influence of the rider's seat, and is totally handless.

The rider must never relinquish control to the horse and become a passenger. He must see to it that the horse always moves in such a way that he can be stopped easily without any temptation to increase the pressure on the reins. Frequent half-halts may be used to restore the balance to prevent the horse from bolting.

The rider should practise bringing the horse to a standstill from walk, trot or canter, on a loose rein, as this is the only way to learn the proper way to influence the horse's back.

CHAPTER TWO

The Essentials of
Training

This chapter explains how to get horses to move actively forwards, on the aids, and straight.

If there are deficiencies in these areas then the aiding system will not work, attempts at schooling will be ineffective, and the rider's enjoyment, control and safety will be compromised.

Forward movement is the first quality to instil in the horse, and means that the horse should move willingly and easily with the merest indication of an aid. This is the most important requirement because nobody wants to ride horses that are reluctant to move - you might as well get off and walk.

Getting the horse on the aids comes second; this implies getting the horse mentally and physically relaxed, and carrying himself properly so he can move easily according to his rider's wishes.

All horses have a degree of one-sidedness. Not only must the rider see to it that his horse does not move in a crooked manner, but also he must plan the schooling so that any unilateral stiffness or weakness is ultimately alleviated. In the course of time the horse will then gradually become easier to straighten.

Active Forward Movement

The Requirement

The first requirement we have of any riding horse is that he should move actively without the rider having to exert himself. Strictly speaking, in equestrian terms, **forward movement** is understood nowadays to refer to the horse's desire to move forwards rather than to actual forward progression. Hence the horse must be thinking **forwards** even when halting or stepping backwards! This has always been a requirement, but this interpretation of the word 'forward' is a modern one. The old masters associated the word literally with gaining ground to the front, and stated that the horse must always make a little

The rising trot is particularly useful with novice horses. It helps to relax them and it encourages the development of free active paces. *(Photo: John Birt)*

forward progress in everything he does unless he is at a halt or reining back or performing some more elaborate exercise to the rear. This still holds true today.

The riding horse must have the capacity for gathering up the power in his quarters so that upward transitions, either within the pace or to another pace, can be effected with the merest indication of an aid; but he should move slowly and majestically. This is what is understood by the term **impulsion.** Strangely, capacity for fast work does not indicate that the horse can move actively forwards in the way that is required in a riding horse. Speed merely indicates that the horse can move his legs quickly. In classical circles the racehorse is not considered to have much impulsion.

All the advanced movements in riding are created from the energy given by the horse's natural urge to move forwards, and without it there is little that can be done with him.

Rider Interference

Usually forward movement is not difficult to achieve because horses actually enjoy moving about. Should the horse be reluctant to move, the first thing to check is the rider's position and motion in the saddle. If the rider cannot conform to the motion of the horse's back, then moving about will no longer be a pleasant experience for the horse. The rider will then need to use strong aids to overcome the resistance that he himself is creating, and he too will cease to enjoy the ride. A great deal of effort should be devoted to perfecting the seat of the beginner because everything in riding depends on it.

Problems sometimes develop because of an uneducated use of the aids. The rider's legs should never make the horse speed up. Speed is often offered as a means of evading a more controlled energy output. Speed is not a requirement in the riding horse. It is not an acceptable response to any of the rider's aids and should be prevented by means of a firm half-halt. It is also important to know that the reins must not be used to bring about downward transitions.

Forward movement can be destroyed by trying to force the horse into a certain position. It is wrong to use force to raise or lower the horse's neck, or to make him flex at the poll. The rider's main concern should never be the shaping of his horse. If the head is carried too high, for example, it would not help to bring it down with draw reins – this would be treating the symptom instead of the cause. The horse must instead be re-educated to raise his back and engage his hind legs so he can carry the rider properly. When he can do this he will automatically lower his head.

The double bridle should not be used until the horse can perform all transitions and all lateral work with the rider holding the reins of the snaffle in one hand. Although the curb may encourage an attractive head carriage, if it is used too soon the danger is that it will interfere with the action of the hocks and the horse will shorten his stride.

There are some contemporary misunderstandings regarding the way the horse should be ridden 'from the leg into the hand'. It is not good to compress the horse longitudinally throughout his frame because this results in blocking the shoulders and interferes with the freedom of movement. In contrast to longitudinal shortening, the classical system produces a lowering of the haunches which gives the impression that the horse is being ridden uphill. This lightens the forehand and renders him much easier to ride.

The Lazy Horse

Some horses are naturally lazy, and as such are not ideally suited for use as riding horses because the demands in terms of energy output exceed their natural inclinations.

It is quite common to find riding-school horses that require so much effort to get them to move that the rider cannot help but compromise his position in the saddle. Some of these horses are lazy by nature and are therefore unsuitable mounts for riders who wish to learn the finer points of equitation. Other horses have been spoiled by a combination of inappropriate, boring repetitive work and frequent riding by inexperienced riders whom they find uncomfortable to carry.

With lazy horses the rider may feel the need for spurs. These should be avoided if possible, because they are needed in later stages of training to enable the aids to be refined, and to improve the cadence so that the horse becomes more springy and bouncy in his action. The use of spurs is permitted, however, if they enable the rider to dispense with an uncivilised or violent use of the whip. Lazy horses should be given a greater variety of work to keep them interested, and their schooling can often be done while hacking out so they don't even realise they are working. Frequent transitions will help to make the horse concentrate and keep him energetic.

Some of the joy of movement can be restored to the jaded horse by lungeing or long-reining.

When practising more advanced exercises the horse will sometimes hold back as an evasion, and he will refuse to move freely forwards. This must not be allowed to become a habit. The remedy is to return to easier exercises and to drive the horse forwards again. Sometimes hacking out or jumping will renew the flagging impulsion. The rider may find it easier if he adopts a forward seat. He can return to the classical position once the impulsion has been restored.

Physiological Problems

Some horses do not move actively because of physiological problems – back pain is one example, or because of discomfort through badly fitting tack. Energy output can also be affected by illness, incorrect feeding or lack of physical fitness.

Putting the Horse on the Aids

To be 'on the aids' the horse has to carry himself in such a way that he is immediately able to comply with the rider's wishes. For this he must be mentally and physically relaxed, and he must use the muscles of his top-line properly so that he carries the rider on a braced back, and stretches to seek a contact with the bit.

The horse's movements should be supple, and he should be comfortable to ride. He must not rush along with tense, hurried steps, but should take long, slow, active strides. Depending on his stage of training the horse must engage his hind legs to a lesser or greater extent. An advanced horse must also tilt his pelvis and lower his haunches. The horse must not support the rider's weight on his shoulders, hollowing his back and allowing his hind legs to trail behind. His head must hang from the muscles in the top of his neck and must not be propped up by the lower neck muscles.

The way the horse carries his head and neck will indicate the proportion of weight that he carries on his haunches. As his balance improves he will develop a higher head carriage with a gracefully arched neck. The young horse will show a much lower neck position which the rider must not try to raise by any means other than seeking to engage the hind legs and thereby lower the haunches a little more. The horse must never hold himself in a shortened frame in 'self collection', but must always be ready to lengthen himself.

When the horse is not carrying himself properly he may be **behind the bit** or **above the bit**. The following two sections explain some of the possible causes and offer some guidance on how to get the horse **on the bit**, but first of all a few general words of advice are in order. Check that the saddle, bridle and rider are causing no discomfort. If the horse is young and his back is not yet strong, ride with slightly shorter stirrups and rise to the trot; but do not lean forwards. Generally it is better to keep rising to the trot until the horse is properly on the aids. It is easiest to put the horse on the aids at trot first, then canter, and finally at the walk.

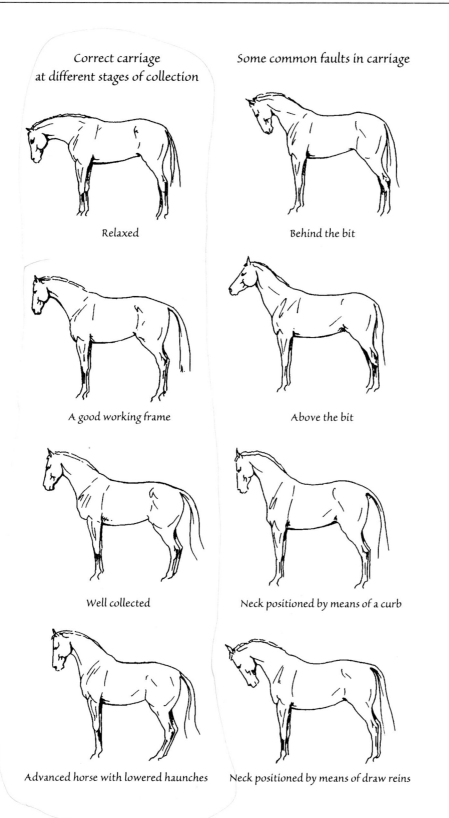

Correct carriage
at different stages of collection

Some common faults in carriage

Relaxed

Behind the bit

A good working frame

Above the bit

Well collected

Neck positioned by means of a curb

Advanced horse with lowered haunches

Neck positioned by means of draw reins

Horse Behind the Bit

This horse gives way at the poll and tucks his chin into his chest. In this position the rider has no means of controlling the engagement of the hind legs because there is nothing to drive them up to. Some causes and remedies are listed below:

♦ The horse may be tired or weak. By dropping behind the bit he can avoid the effort of working correctly. The horse should be given shorter periods of work and not driven beyond his capabilities.

♦ The rider may have his hands too widely separated. This gives a hard unyielding contact from which dropping behind the bit is the horse's only escape. The rider's hands should be held close together. One of the ultimate objectives of schooling is to be able to ride the horse with the reins in one hand.

Behind the bit

Above the bit

Young horse in a correct position

- If the rider uses the reins in a heavy-handed way to set the position of the head and neck, the horse may try to avoid the discomfort by dropping behind the bit.

- The use of draw reins can cause the horse to bend at the third vertebra in the neck instead of at the poll. Once the horse has developed the habit of flexing in this way the condition can be extremely difficult to correct. Even a very experienced trainer will have trouble rectifying the fault.

- Sometimes the problem can be cured by shortening up the reins so that some pressure is put on the horse's mouth regardless of how far he tries to drop behind the bit. His attempts at evading the contact will be frustrated, and he will probably try to thrust his nose forward to pull the reins out of the rider's hands. This reaction should be encouraged, and he should be rewarded whenever he stretches forwards. If he drops behind the bit again the rider should attempt to re-establish a contact and repeat the process.

- Being behind the bit can be due to previous errors in training rather than a problem with the present rider. A general remedy is to drive vigorously so the horse has to stretch forward with his head and neck. As he stretches forwards he must be given a light, comfortable contact.

- Young horses often carry their heads low with the line of the face behind the vertical. Although superficially this gives the appearance of being behind the bit it is quite different. It is not a fault at all because there is no deliberate evasion – they are not backing away from the contact. In the course of time these horses will become stronger and will then be able to raise their necks.

Horse Above the Bit

This is far more common. The horse fixes his poll rigidly in place so it won't bend at all. He drops his back and stops engaging the hind legs. There are a number of remedies to choose from according to circumstance. The first two are rather crude, and they do nothing to work the haunches, so they must be followed by one or more of the other alternatives. They may be of particular value to less-experienced riders who have difficulties achieving results with the other techniques.

♦ The rider stretches his arms out in front of him, and raises them up high, putting some tension on the reins to pull the bit up into the corners of the horse's mouth. The horse should react against the pressure by plunging his head downwards. The rider yields and rewards his horse.

♦ The rider places one hand palm upwards in front of the withers, with the middle finger separating the reins. He slides this hand upwards towards his chin, and repeats the process with alternate hands so there is a continual upward sliding effect. This should cause the horse to lower his head, at which point the rider yields and rewards his horse. This technique can only be used with plain leather reins.

♦ When the horse stretches his neck out and pokes his nose the usual cause is an indefinite or unsteady contact given by the rider. The latter should rest his hands, one on each thigh, as if the horse were in side-reins. This gives the horse a comfortable frame to work in, steadies the rider's hands, and joins the bit to the rider's seat more effectively. The horse is driven vigorously forwards into the contact. The inside rein may be vibrated to encourage the horse to yield. The hands may alternatively be rested on the front of the saddle or on the horse's neck. When the horse yields and comes on the bit the rider must hold his hands close together as otherwise the horse might drop behind the bit. It is most important to understand that this technique is not meant to encourage the rider to fix the horse's head in position. Resting the hands is a temporary remedy for unsteady hands, and the real cure comes from driving forwards into a properly defined contact.

♦ If the horse is hollow-backed and way above the bit, trot him in circles. Rest the inside hand on the thigh, and drive vigorously with the inside leg. Yield the outside rein in time with the movement - release the contact and stroke his neck each time the outside shoulder moves forwards. The horse is obliged to flex the joints of his inside hind leg. To avoid the discomfort he arches his back and drops his head - at which point the circle can be widened and the horse rewarded.

♦ If the horse stops engaging and comes above the bit, drive vigorously with legs and whip. Don't forget that the horse needs adequate rest periods.

♦ If the horse loses balance, runs forward and comes above the bit, use a half-halt to re-balance him. Several half-halts may be required in each circuit of the arena.

♦ The horse may not remain on the aids if the rider's hands are unyielding. The rider should yield each rein a little in time with the movement as the shoulder on the same side advances. This yielding is only slight, and not enough to make the rein hang loose.

♦ Several turns on the forehand executed in succession are a very effective way of engaging the inside hind leg, and the horse will very soon lower his head. At this point the rider can ask for a trot and should be able to keep the horse on the aids, at least on small circles.

♦ The exercise of shoulder-in executed on a circle is similarly very effective in keeping the inside hind leg will engaged.

♦ At walk, trot or canter the rider should be able at any time to lower the horse's poll to the level of his withers. Never dismount until the horse lowers his head. Yield the reins alternately and stroke the horse's neck. Wait for the head to be lowered and then dismount as a reward. Eventually the horse will recognise the yielding and neck stroking, and will lower his head on demand.

How NOT to Put the Horse on the Aids

There are a number of bad techniques which cannot be recommended because they address the symptoms rather than the cause of the problem and are likely to do more harm than good. These are listed below:

♦ **Pulling on the reins** This tightens the muscles in the horse's neck, and in the rider's arms, creating tension and stiffness. It prevents the full engagement of the hind legs, so the horse pushes himself forwards instead of carrying himself.

♦ **Use of curbs and pelhams** With these it is possible to force the horse to carry his head and neck elegantly, but they have no useful effect on the back or hindquarters. They cause tension instead of comfort and relaxation. Correct head carriage cannot be forced; it has to be a natural by-product obtained when the horse uses his hindquarters and back correctly. The use of curbs on advanced horses is a different matter altogether.

♦ **Use of draw reins/running reins** These should only be used in exceptional circumstances, and by experienced trainers; they are not for novices. The danger is that they can force the head and neck into a caricature of the carriage required of an advanced horse. The horse may become broken at the third vertebra instead of flexing at the poll, and drop behind the bit. It is acceptable to use draw reins to prevent a deviation from the correct position when a new exercise is being taught, but it is not acceptable to use them in an attempt to correct a faulty position.

♦ **Help from the ground** A trainer on the ground walks beside the ridden horse holding one rein in each hand. By holding one rein and vibrating the other he encourages the horse to flex at the poll. The rider then attempts to maintain this flexion unaided by the trainer. This technique results in poll flexion, but does not raise the back or lower the haunches, and so does not help to get to the root of the problem. Flexion at the poll is not a primary requirement, but unfortunately it is the feature most easily noticed by the casual observer. Rather than use this method it would be better to lunge the horse in side-reins to teach him to accept a correct contact.

♦ **Active use of the reins** The rider continually vibrates or fiddles with the reins and succeeds in frustrating the horse's attempts at lifting his head above the bit. This does not solve the problem because it does not remove the cause of the horse wanting to go above the bit. Really the rider should use more leg or change to another exercise, such as the shoulder-in, to encourage more engagement.

♦ **Change of rider's position** The rider leans forwards and holds his hands low down on the horse's neck. Again this just works the front of the horse. By leaning forwards the rider loses the use of his seat and has no means of raising the horse's back. The forward seat may be adopted for training over cavaletti, and it is the proper seat to use when riding cross-country and jumping, but it is of little value when working on the flat.

Straightening the Horse

The horse must be straight [handwritten annotation]

Crookedness in the horse has been recognised as a serious fault for hundreds of years. Back in the seventeenth century the Duke of Newcastle wrote: 'I take it to be a great vice, when a horse does not go as well to one hand as to the other; and I have seen very few that do so; but if you punctually follow my method, your horses will go to perfection, and as well to one hand as the other, so that you will never see any difference.'

There are three important considerations relating to straightness:

♦ In single-track work the hind feet must follow directly in the tracks of the fore feet rather than stepping to one side to avoid the discomfort of carrying and propelling the weight.

♦ When moving on a circular track the horse must bend himself in a continuous curve towards the direction in which he is moving; the tighter the circle, the tighter the bend required. This involves curving the neck, turning the shoulders and engaging the inside hind leg. With the exception of the neck and tail, the spine of the horse is relatively rigid and is capable of very little lateral flexion.

♦ The horse must not lean towards one shoulder or one hip so that one limb bears more weight than its neighbour.

All horses by nature tend to be crooked to some extent, and if proper attention is not given to these matters then the musculature will develop asymmetrically and the problem will become chronic. A horse is chronically crooked if any part of his body is stiffer or weaker than the corresponding part on the other side. In this case a longer period of time devoted to appropriate remedial gymnastic exercises will be needed before straightness can be established.

When the horse is equally easy to ride on either rein then he is straight. The straight horse turns right and left with equal facility, his hind limbs are equally well developed in their powers of flexion, weight

Dr Reiner Klimke displays a correct bend to the left. The bend is continuous from poll to tail. *(Photo: John Birt)*

support and propulsion, and he takes an even contact with the bit on both sides of his mouth. Crookedness will be more marked at times when the horse is fresh or excited.

One-sidedness reveals itself to the rider in a number of different ways, not the least of which is that the contact with the bit feels firmer on the stiff side, so much so that the rider may pull the bit out of the mouth on that side by as much as two inches. Consequently many riders imagine that the seat of crookedness lies in the mouth; some very eminent riders have been misguided in this way. It is easy to prove that the problem is not confined to the mouth: fix the reins to cavesson rings instead of to the bit, and the contact will feel just as uneven as it did before!

Causes of Crookedness

♦ Congenital asymmetry.

♦ Because of a natural right- or left-handedness, the horse has a tendency to favour certain limbs.

♦ When moving alongside a wall the horse may lean towards it with his shoulders so that the hip and shoulder nearest the wall are equidistant from it.

♦ When working on small circles the horse may lean towards the inside shoulder to avoid bending his body.

♦ The horse soon discovers that he does not have to work so hard if he goes crookedly, so he tries to do so as an evasion.

♦ Always leading in hand from the same side; always mounting from the same side.

♦ Allowing the horse to choose his favourite leading leg at canter regardless of the aids.

♦ Always rising to the trot on the same diagonal.

♦ Rider sitting crookedly.

Signs of Crookedness

♦ The horse takes a strong contact on one side of his mouth, and a light contact on the other.

♦ The horse flexes in one direction more easily than the other. On the stiff side his neck muscles are firm, whilst those on the hollow side are slack and less well developed.

♦ When going large around the arena the horse cuts the corners to avoid flexing or carrying weight on the inside hind leg. This can happen on either the stiff side or the hollow side.

♦ When riding circles on the hollow side the horse is reluctant to carry any weight on the inside hind leg. Some horses will fall in towards the inside shoulder and execute a very small circle or a pirouette; some will take too much weight on their outside shoulder and carry too little with their inside hind leg, and their haunches will turn slightly inwards. Other horses will try to whip round and turn away in the other direction.

♦ When riding circles on the stiff side the horse has difficulty in flexing his inside hind leg. Some horses will try to execute a larger circle than the rider requires. If the rider were to let go of the reins the horse would cease the circle and turn away in the other direction. Other horses will remain counter-flexed and lean into the circle, taking the weight on the inside shoulder.

♦ When riding on a circular track the horse may bend himself in a discontinuous curve. Usually part of the neck is bent in the wrong direction and the head is brought into line by means of a kink just before the faulty curve, often at the withers. Sometimes both the neck and the body have an incorrect bend but the rider may be fooled because of the angle at the withers.

♦ When riding in straight lines, the quarters fall in towards the hollow side, and the horse drifts diagonally forwards towards the shoulder on the stiff side.

♦ On the hollow side the hind leg takes long low strides, whilst on the stiff side the stride is shorter but the hock rises higher.

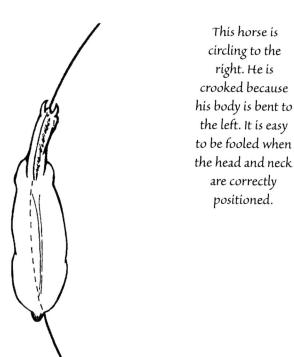

This horse is circling to the right. He is crooked because his body is bent to the left. It is easy to be fooled when the head and neck are correctly positioned.

♦ The horse strikes off into canter more easily on the side whose shoulder carries the lesser weight.

♦ At shoulder-in on the hollow side the horse will lean onto his outside shoulder, take too little weight on his inside hind leg, and he will bring the neck in rather than the shoulder.

♦ At shoulder-in on the stiff side the horse will not engage the inside hind leg sufficiently, and the ply of his body will be insufficient.

♦ At haunches-in on the hollow side the horse will bring his haunches in at too great an angle. He will keep his body too straight and avoid taking weight on the inside hind leg.

♦ At haunches-in on the stiff side the horse will not bring the haunches in sufficiently, and he will have difficulty bending his body and engaging the inside hind leg.

♦ At half-pass towards the hollow side the horse will move freely but the crossing of the outside hind leg will be insufficient.

♦ At half-pass towards the stiff side the horse will not move very

Correct positioning

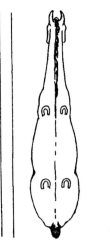

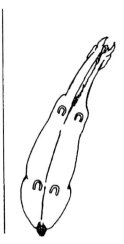

On a single track

At shoulder-in

At haunches-in

Positional faults

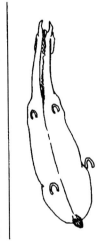

Incorrect neck bending

Bringing the neck in to evade
the shoulder-in

Crooked horse
on a single track
with disengaged
right hind leg

freely. The outside hind leg will cross over but he will try to counter-flex his body and leg-yield instead.

♦ After dismounting the rider may notice marks on the saddle which show that the horse has succeeded in carrying him more to one side than the other.

Summary of Requirements

♦ Keep the horse's shoulders upright and directly in front of his haunches.

♦ Increase the ply of the horse's body to the stiff side.

♦ Relax the neck muscles on the stiff side, and build up the neck muscles on the hollow side.

♦ Increase the engagement of the hind leg on the stiff side, and the weight-bearing capacity of the hind leg on the hollow side.

♦ Encourage the horse to take a firmer contact with the bit on the hollow side, and to stop leaning on the bit on the stiff side.

Techniques for Straightening the Horse

Establishing straightness can be a slow process, taking months or even years. This is because the horse has to get into the habit of carrying himself properly, and he has to build up the muscles that will enable him to do so.

Generally it is not a good idea to work more on the stiff side than the hollow side. Both sides have problems which need attention.

REIN CONTACT

One of the most effective strategies is never to take a firm contact on the rein of the stiff side.

Some horses take such an uneven contact on the bit that it is almost impossible to get a contact at all on the hollow side. The remedy is to walk the horse, holding only the rein of the hollow side. He will eventually tire of turning his head to avoid the contact, and will stretch his neck and find the bit. This should be rewarded by yielding and by stroking his neck.

When circling towards the stiff side the rider will be tempted to take a firm contact on the inside rein to make the horse bend in the correct direction and to make him turn onto a small enough circle. When circling towards the hollow side the temptation will be to take a firm contact on the outside rein to prevent the horse from falling in.

If the rider does take up this contact on the stiff side then it will give the horse something to lean on. He will continue to move crookedly and one side of his mouth will become deadened into the bargain. In time the horse will get even more one-sided. Instead the rider should use a stronger inside leg and more inside seat pressure combined with a contact on the rein of the hollow side. This will encourage the horse to use his hind limbs more evenly.

The straight horse can be ridden between the inside leg and the outside rein; but this does not apply to the crooked horse. The rider should always encourage the horse to take a contact on the soft side.

A COMMON PROBLEM

Perhaps the most common instance of crookedness is seen when the horse allows his quarters to fall in. This usually occurs at canter. When the horse leans towards the wall with his shoulders in this way he should be straightened by bringing his shoulders in with both reins, supported by pressure from the outside leg - the aids are similar to those that would be used for a step or two of a turn on the haunches at walk. The rider must not use his inside leg behind the girth to push the haunches out to the shoulders. This would not make the inside hind leg engage properly or carry its full share of weight, and the horse would remain crooked.

The counter-canter is a good exercise to practise with the horse whose quarters fall in at canter. At counter-canter there is usually no evasion.

The haunches are more likely to fall in when working towards the hollow side. This is due to weakness in the inside hind leg. Frequent transitions into canter with the stiff side leading will help to strengthen this weakness because then it is the weaker leg that is obliged to propel the horse forwards into canter.

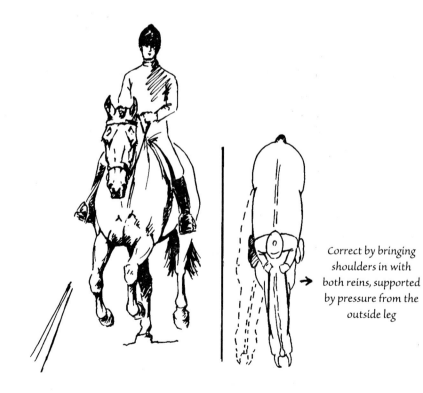

Correct by bringing shoulders in with both reins, supported by pressure from the outside leg

Quarters falling in at canter.

USE OF LATERAL WORK

In addition to encouraging engagement and suppling the shoulders, the shoulder-in is also marvellous for its effectiveness in straightening the horse. When practised towards the hollow side it helps the horse to angulate his body in the direction opposite to the one he prefers, and it obliges him to carry weight on his inside hind leg.

If when working on circles the horse crosses his inside hind leg over the outside one, the exercise of shoulder-out on the same circle will be beneficial.

To straighten the horse who leans onto his inside shoulder when circling towards the stiff side, work on larger circles in a slight shoulder-in, or 'shoulder-fore' position. To prevent counter-flexion, temporarily fix the inside hand on the saddle or the thigh, and release the pressure on the outside rein until the shoulders straighten up again. The horse should then be encouraged to take a contact on the outside rein. If this method is unsuccessful take a contact on the outside rein, and combined with pressure from the inside leg on the girth, take and give gently with the inside rein in the direction of the outside breast. When the shoulders have been made upright they will from time to time tend to lean in again. This can be nipped in the bud by raising the inside hand so that the rein acts, without pulling, in the direction of the rider's outside breast, and by simultaneously increasing the pressure of the inside leg. It is often easier to straighten the horse if his head and neck are first given a lower position.

When working in the direction of the stiff side, shoulder-in helps to improve the lateral bending, encourages the horse to take a contact with the bit on the hollow side, and counteracts his tendency to drift towards the shoulder of the stiff side. Haunches-in to the stiff side is a particularly effective exercise because it encourages angulation and lateral bending which are opposite to those preferred by the horse.

When working in the direction of the hollow side the rider must take care in haunches-in that the horse bends correctly and carries enough weight on the inside hind leg. If the horse moves along at an angle

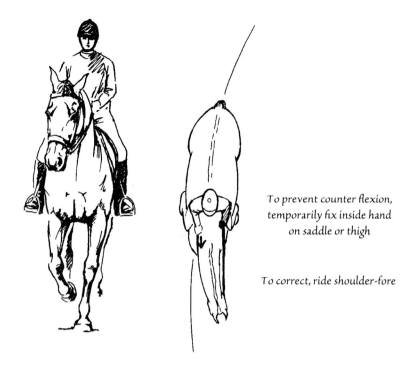

To prevent counter flexion,
temporarily fix inside hand
on saddle or thigh

To correct, ride shoulder-fore

Correcting the horse who leans towards the stiff side.

without bending his body or loading the inside hind leg then the exercise is best avoided as it will only encourage crookedness. At shoulder-in the rider must be careful that the horse does not overbend his neck towards the hollow side, lean towards his outside shoulder, and take too firm a contact on the outside rein. Sometimes this fault is easier to correct by interrupting the shoulder-in, riding a volte, and then proceeding with a new shoulder-in.

When riding half-passes towards the stiff side, first position the horse as for a shoulder-in. This will discourage him from leaning on the inside shoulder and counter-flexing. A half-pass ridden at an energetic rising trot will increase the horse's facility in moving towards the stiff side.

When riding half-passes towards the hollow side ride them at a steep angle so they are more like a full pass. This will increase the crossing of the outside hind leg. Starting from a haunches-in position can also increase the crossing of the outside hind leg. After practising lateral exercises such as these it is important to ride actively forwards again to restore the impulsion and regularity.

ADDITIONAL HINTS FOR THE RIDER

Horses can be remarkably cunning at evading the rider's efforts to straighten them. Often it can be an advantage to carry two schooling whips.

It is very important to be aware of how evenly the horse distributes the weight and how symmetrically he moves. Only by becoming more sensitive to the imperfections can the rider hope to correct them. At first, while performing the easier exercises the rider may not be aware of any crookedness, but as he progresses to more advanced work he will begin to notice that the horse carries himself quite differently when working on opposite reins. Then if the rider returns to the easier exercises he will be able to feel that the crookedness does in fact manifest itself at that level: he will have become more sensitive and will be better able to straighten his horse.

CHAPTER THREE

Balance

The term **balance** is generally used in equestrian circles to mean ease and facility of movement; **poise** would probably be a more appropriate word. The ease with which the horse can manœuvre himself depends on balance in the sense that it is directly affected by the distribution of weight over his limbs. This weight distribution, or balance, also affects the grace with which the horse appears to move.

By nature the horse is inclined to carry some two thirds of his weight on the front legs and one third on the hind legs. This is adequate for the wild horse who spends a good deal of time walking about grazing, and has the occasional gallop to escape from danger. The horseman, on the other hand, requires his mount to perform finely controlled and intricate patterns without any awkwardness. For this the horse must take more weight onto his haunches and lighten the burden carried by his forelimbs.

As the horse's balance improves he gains more control of his own body. According to where he places his hind feet on the ground and how he uses his haunches he can modify his rate of progress, change his length of stride, and alter the springiness with which he bounces off the ground. The rider will be able to tap these abilities and will have a very versatile horse at his disposal.

The art of improving the horse's balance consists of teaching him to bend the joints of his hind legs, to lower his haunches, and to raise and lighten his forehand. As a result of this his appearance will improve because he will develop a gracefully arched neck. He will also give the impression that he is going uphill. This chapter explains how these objectives can be achieved.

Testing for Balance

A good test of balance is the ease with which downward transitions can be ridden. A well-balanced horse should be able to halt easily from an extended trot or an extended canter.

If the horse is poorly balanced, with too much weight on the forehand, then he will lean on the bit and be inclined to rush ahead. He will lose rhythm when changing from collection to extension and vice versa, and downward transitions will be jolting and uncomfortable.

In extreme cases the unbalanced horse will bolt and run away like an avalanche because he has so little control over the effects that the natural laws of motion have on his body. A stronger bit will not help: pressure on the rein gives the horse something to lean against and impedes the engagement of the hind leg on the same side. This in turn destroys the balance and puts the horse even more on the forehand.

Techniques for Improving Balance

The rider should be warned that he cannot expect to improve his horse by using the reins to lift the horse's head into the required position, or by using a bit that forces the horse to carry himself differently. Such methods would not compel him to take more weight on his haunches, and they would encourage him to stiffen his back. Very likely the balance would deteriorate.

The horse has to be gymnasticised so he can bend the joints of his hind legs and collect himself. When he can do this he will automatically raise his neck into a better position.

Correct training on classical lines will always improve the horse's balance. Here, Arthur Kottas rides an advanced Lipizzan. The stallion easily maintains a high degree of collection without any apparent exertion from his rider. *(Photo: Andreas Jarc)*

♦ **Lateral bending** All the exercises which encourage lateral bending – circles, voltes, serpentines, shoulder-in, haunches-in, and half-pass etc. – have a beneficial effect because they encourage the bending of the joints in the hind legs. Consequently the muscles associated with these joints are strengthened and the haunches are able to carry more weight. Shoulder-in strengthens the hocks, haunches-in strengthens the stifles, and half-pass supples the hips.

♦ **Lengthening and shortening strides** Frequent changes from collection to extension and vice versa at trot and at canter are an excellent means of teaching the horse to control his balance. They improve his capacity for longitudinal flexion, which will enable him to lower his haunches and raise his forehand. These exercises can be practised very early in the horse's training. Contact with the bit and rhythm must remain unaltered throughout the transitions. If the horse is allowed to increase the tempo during extensions he will stop swinging his back and come off the aids, and this will not help his balance.

♦ **Transitions to another pace** Direct transitions such as halt to trot or canter to halt, for example, not only serve as an indication of the horse's capacity for controlling his balance but also they help to improve it by making him more collected.

♦ **The half-halt** Whenever the horse appears to be losing balance and getting more on the forehand, a half-halt should be used. The half-halt is the most important re-balancing exercise of all, and arguably the most useful exercise in the whole of classical riding. As many as one hundred half-halts might be performed in the space of a half-hour schooling session.

♦ **Hill work** Downward transitions performed on gentle downhill slopes are an excellent way to encourage the hind legs to step further forwards, provided of course that they are brought about by the use of the rider's seat. This is an exercise for the more advanced horse.

♦ **The horse's loins** Once the horse's hind limbs have been strengthened by lateral work his loins can be strengthened. The exercises that will accomplish this are the counter-canter and the rein-back. The horse will then be able to develop greater powers of collection.

♦ **Greater collection** When the horse can work easily at collected trot and collected canter, these paces can be collected even further to produce the 'school trot' and the 'school canter'. At this level of collection the horse should go no faster than a man's walking speed, and the distance covered at each stride should be half that covered at the usual collected paces. At the school trot and school canter the contact with the bit should be very light.

♦ **The horse's pelvis** When the school paces have been mastered it will be time to work towards the piaffe and the canter pirouette. These exercises will encourage the horse to tilt his pelvis so he can take even more weight on his haunches, and this will bring about the ultimate development of his balance.

CHAPTER FOUR

Resistances

Every rider gets into difficulty from time to time because his horse will not comply with his wishes.

The horse has a variety of means at his disposal for resisting the rider's demands. They range from the mild and passive to the active and violent. The horse might do something as simple as holding himself in such a position that he cannot perform the required exercise, or he might try to harm or unseat his rider.

The more serious and dangerous forms of resistance are often caused by a lack of understanding between horse and rider, and poor horsemanship in general. They can arise if the milder resistances are not properly understood and dealt with. Every rider must know how to cope with resistances, and the first step is to understand what the possible causes might be.

Common Causes of Resistance

♦ **Lack of understanding** The horse does not comprehend the rider's instructions. Horses must always be introduced to the aids gradually. It would, for example, be just as useless to kick the sides of an uneducated horse to make him move as it would be to shout at a foreigner to make him understand.

♦ **Excessive demands** The rider makes demands which exceed the horse's capabilities. The horse may have temporary difficulties caused by stiffness, weakness or fatigue.

♦ **Faulty aiding** The rider's position or aids restrict the horse's movements so that he is unable to do as he is bid. The rider will probably accentuate the aids in an attempt to overcome the resistance, but he may also increase those signals that prevent the desired effect.

♦ **Fear** The horse is frightened to comply with the rider's demands. This is a common cause of nappiness. The rider must try to overcome the horse's fear. In the course of time the horse will gain confidence in the rider's judgment and the problem will disappear.

♦ **Pain** The horse is suffering from pain or discomfort which makes proper response to the aids difficult.

♦ **Laziness** The horse is lazy and tries to avoid work in order to make life easier for himself.

♦ **Habit** The horse has discovered how he can evade the rider's aids, and has scored a major victory in learning how to get the better of the rider.

The rider must always remain calm and conduct himself properly; he must never act rashly or he may start a downhill slide into ultimate defeat for himself and victory for the horse. This should be avoided at all costs, because once the horse realises how much power he really has over his rider he will always be liable to take advantage.

The best way to cope with resistances is to avoid them altogether. Provided the training is planned in a systematic way so that the demands on the horse are increased only gradually, he will be able to cope with his work easily and he will not resist. All horses must be treated as individuals, and when difficulties are encountered the schooling must be tailored to the specific needs.

It is the trainer's duty to understand his equine pupil and to make his education a pleasant experience. The riding school must not become a battle ground; the horse must be considered a friend, not an adversary.

CHAPTER FIVE

Progressive Lateral Work

The term 'lateral' is applied to any movement in which the horse progresses sideways and forwards, at an angle to the direction he is facing.

At first sight it might appear pointless to want the horse to move in such a fashion, and since some of the movements are not performed at liberty, their validity could, with some justification, be questioned. They have been included in the training programme for hundreds of years because they have proved to be tremendously beneficial to the physical development of the horse. Some of the lateral movements should be regarded purely as gymnastic exercises; they are a means to an end rather than an objective in themselves. Other movements, such as the canter pirouette, are more natural to the horse, and have some practical use and some artistic merit in addition to their potential for physical exercise.

The horse is ready to start lateral work as soon as he can respond correctly to the rider's seat when performing all the simple transitions up the scale from a standstill to walk, on to trot, and then canter, and back down again to trot, walk, and halt. Normally the young horse will be ready to start in his second year of training.

Early Beginnings

The Turn on the Forehand

The first lateral movement for the horse to master is the turn on the forehand. It can be performed only at a walk, but can be started from either a halt or a walk. As an exercise it has very limited potential, but it does pave the way for more useful movements.

When performing a turn on the forehand to the right, for example, the horse moves his quarters clockwise away from the rider's right leg in a circle, or a part circle, around his own right fore foot, which stays at the centre of the circle. The right side is known as the inside in this case.

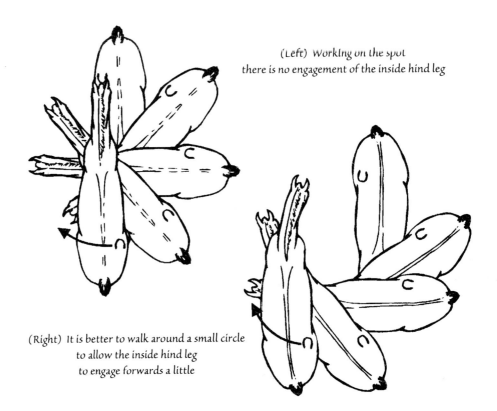

(Left) Working on the spot
there is no engagement of the inside hind leg

(Right) It is better to walk around a small circle
to allow the inside hind leg
to engage forwards a little

Half turn on the forehand.

The inside fore foot should continue to step up and down in a tiny circle in the rhythm of the walk, and the horse should be given a good bend to the inside. If he is kept straight or if the inside fore foot is kept moving exactly on the spot without gaining a little ground at each step, then the exercise will be detrimental. This is because the inside hind leg will be made to step sideways rather than engaging sideways and forwards, and consequently the joints will not be encouraged to bend and take the weight.

The horse should be given some preparation in the stable by being taught to move his quarters over when a hand is pressed against his side. If this is not done, he may not realise that he is supposed to move away from the pressure of the rider's leg. It is important to understand that this is a trained response rather than a natural one. The horse cannot escape from the rider's leg pressure by moving sideways because he carries his rider with him.

The Leg-Yield

After the turn on the forehand many riders progress to leg-yielding. For a leg-yield to the left, for example, the horse would be virtually straight except for a slight flexion to the right at the poll, and would move diagonally forwards and sideways away from the rider's right leg. The leg-yield can be ridden at walk or trot.

This fashionable movement is a modern invention, and is the subject of some controversy. It is not well regarded by the classical purist because it does not encourage the haunches to engage: the inside hind leg moves too much sideways and not sufficiently forwards into a position where it could participate in weight support. Consequently the exercise is not academically sound, and if ridden as it is supposed to be it will be detrimental to the horse's development.

Trainers who do recommend the leg-yield invariably give their horses a little more bend and succeed it obtaining some engagement with the inside hind leg. When ridden this way the exercise begins to act more like a shoulder-in, and it can then be very useful for loosening up a stiff horse. Another advantage of the leg-yield is that it gives the novice rider some practice in manœuvring his horse, and is a good preparation for learning to ride the shoulder-in, which is one of the most beneficial exercises that can be practised with the horse.

Useful Gymnastic Exercises

The Shoulder-in

La Guérinière is usually credited with inventing the shoulder-in, in the eighteenth century. It was previously described, however, in the seventeenth century by the Duke of Newcastle, who used the exercise on a circular track, and it was later adapted by La Guérinière for use on straight lines.

This exercise is one of the most useful available to the trainer. It supples the shoulders, encourages engagement and strengthens the hocks, and it can be used to straighten the horse by replacing the forehand in front of an evading hind leg.

The principle of the shoulder-in is that the horse is made to curve his body round in front of the inside hind leg so that this hind leg does more than its usual amount of work and is the prime pushing limb for propelling the horse along. The exercise cannot be called a shoulder-in if the rider achieves it by pulling the horse in with the inside rein, as this would have a detrimental effect on the action of the inside hind leg, which must have the freedom to be grounded in the best position for weight carriage and propulsion.

There are some arguments over how far the shoulders should be brought in. Opinions are divided between those who recommend a

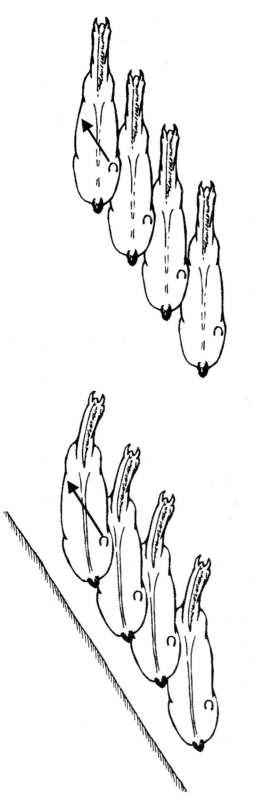

Leg-yield left.

Shoulder-in right.

The shoulder-in is superior to the leg-yield because it encourages the inside hind leg to engage well forwards.

three-track shoulder-in and those who favour bringing the shoulders further in so that the horse makes four tracks on the ground. The most important consideration is the action of the inside hind leg. So long as this continues to engage properly, the shoulders can be brought in to any required degree. If they are brought in too far, however, the hind leg will have to move too much sideways, and the exercise will no longer be beneficial. If the shoulders are brought in only a small amount the position is known as 'shoulder-fore'.

The shoulder-in can be performed at walk or trot. At canter the horse can only bring the shoulders in as far as the shoulder-fore position, and at canter this is known as the 'plié'.

Shoulder-in and shoulder-out can be practised on straight lines or on a circular track. Shoulder-out on the circle is easy to ride, puts weight on the haunches, and loosens the shoulders, which have the greater distance to travel. At walk the size of the circle can be reduced if required until the horse performs a counter-flexed turn on the haunches around his outside hind leg.

Shoulder-in on the circle loosens the haunches, which have more ground to cover than the shoulders, but it puts more weight on the forehand than when the exercise is ridden on the straight line. Shoulder-fore and plié can be used with advantage in all turns and circles as the proper bend will then be assured and some assistance will be given to the engagement of the inside hind leg.

The Haunches-in and the Half-Pass

When the horse has mastered the shoulder-in he can learn the haunches-in. Haunches-in and haunches-out can be ridden at walk, trot or canter, and like the shoulder-in can be performed on a straight line or on a circle. At haunches-out on a circle at walk the size of the circle can be reduced if required until the horse performs a counter-flexed turn on the forehand around his outside foreleg.

In this picture of the haunches-in to the left, the engagement of the right hind leg is particularly obvious. The horse – Olympic Cocktail, ridden by Anky van Grunsven – is well rounded and shows a good bend to the left. *(Photo: John Birt)*

Practising haunches-in along the wall at canter is not advisable because the horse is always ready to let his haunches drift in at canter and the exercise is likely to encourage him to move crookedly. Haunches-out at canter is a much better exercise.

It is worth explaining here that some of the terminology can be confusing, and it can be difficult to visualise the exercises. At canter the horse must always be bent towards the side of the leading leg. When riding haunches-out to the left at canter, the horse would be bent to the left in a left lead canter, and the wall would be on his left side. His haunches would be closer to the wall than his shoulders, which would be on the inner track. Some people might prefer to think of it as a haunches-out at counter-canter. Strictly speaking this would be erroneous thinking because there can be no such thing as a counter-canter on a straight line; there can only be a left lead canter or a right lead canter.

As with the shoulder-in there are disagreements over how far the haunches should be brought in. A diagram in the British Horse Society's book of Dressage Rules shows a four-track exercise. The haunches-in is closely related to the half-pass, and there are those who consider them to be the same thing but call it a half-pass when it is ridden on the diagonal, and a haunches-in at all other times. Others distinguish between the two by stating that at haunches-in the forehand does not deviate from the track but travels directly forwards, so that there is no marked crossing of the outside foreleg over in front of the inside one. By contrast, at half-pass the horse's body is straighter and his forehand moves diagonally forwards and sideways. Distinguishing between the movements in this way it is obvious that it does no harm to bring the haunches in too far; the horse merely starts to cross his forelegs and the exercise becomes functionally equivalent to a half-pass.

Haunches-in is a good exercise for strengthening the stifles, whilst the half-pass supples the hips. In both movements the outside hind leg crosses over in front of the inside one, but the inside hind leg must engage forwards and not step out to the side.

The half-pass is usually ridden on the diagonal, but it can also be ridden alongside the wall, either with the head or the tail to the wall, and on the circle, either with the head or the tail to the centre. All these variations are good gymnastic exercises which can be used to work the horse a little more, provided he can already perform similar exercises at haunches-in or haunches-out without any difficulty. Force must never be used to make the horse perform these movements.

The Full Pass

If the half-pass is ridden at a such a steep angle that the horse moves almost directly sideways with scarcely any forward progression, it is known as a 'full pass'. This is easy to ride at a walk, but only a well-schooled horse will manage a good full pass at trot or canter. It is a useful exercise for demonstrating the degree of control that the rider has over his horse. The full pass should not be attempted on a circular track as it would make the inside hind leg disengage and step out sideways away from the horse, and this would not be good for his physical development.

Advanced Lateral Movements

The most difficult lateral movements have both practicality and some artistic merit. They are the passade and the part or full pirouette.

The Passade

The passade is a small about-turn through one hundred and eighty degrees ridden with the haunches in. It can be used when the rider wishes to turn round and return in the direction from whence he came. It can be ridden at walk, trot, or canter. A good preparation is to place

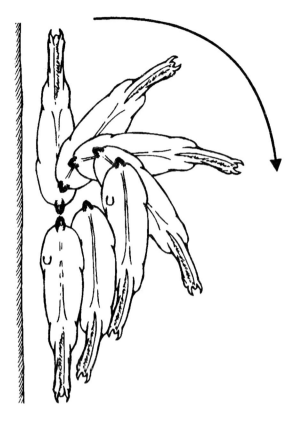

Passade to the right.

the horse in a shoulder-fore position before turning. The inside hind leg must stay well engaged and must move forwards at each step. The actual pattern ridden must be a small semi-circle away from the wall followed by a short half-pass returning to the wall. At walk and canter the passade ridden in this manner is a good preparation for the half-pirouette. At trot it is the closest approximation to the half-pirouette that the horse is able to make.

The Pirouette

The pirouette can be performed at walk or canter. It cannot be performed at the trot, but if the horse is ridden in piaffe then he can be turned on the spot. The walk pirouette can be started from either a walk or a halt. In the latter case it is known as a 'turn on the haunches'. Like the passade the half-pirouette has some practical use as it enables the rider to turn round in a small space without stopping.

Often the pirouette is attempted too early in the horse's education. It should not be practised, even at a walk, until the horse has mastered the half-pass. The reason for this is that the pirouette itself is really a variation on the half-pass: it is a half-pass executed on a very small circle with the haunches to the centre. The horse forms a tangent to a tiny circle whose centre is to the inside of his inside hind foot, and this foot must step forwards around the circumference of the circle. It would be very wrong to turn the horse around a tiny circle whose centre was behind the inside hind foot rather than beside it. This would be the full pass on a circle, and the inside hind foot would be compelled to move sideways and slightly backwards at every step in order to reach the next point on the circumference.

Incorrect turn on the haunches.

The right hind leg is obliged to step sideways and disengage.

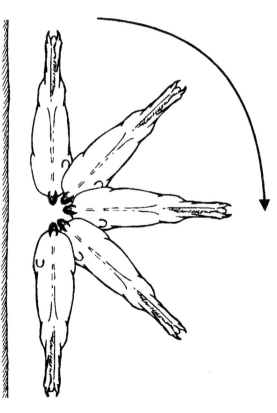

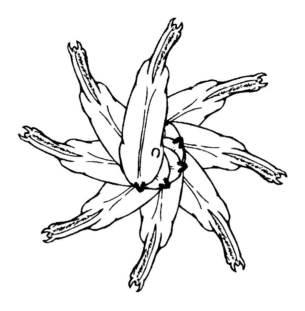

Pirouette right.

A very common fault in the walk pirouette is that it is ridden too slowly. This is caused by insufficient collection, which means the forehand is not liberated and the forelegs are unable to take big steps in the proper rhythm. When the right amount of collection is obtained it is harder for the rider to keep the hind legs stepping in rhythm, and the inside one is liable to remain fixed to the ground. The walk pirouette is a without doubt a very difficult movement to ride well.

The canter pirouette is dealt with in more detail in chapter eight.

CHAPTER SIX

Aids for Bending and Lateral Movements

The purpose of this chapter is to explain, with the aid of some diagrams, how the rider can help the horse to bend and to move laterally. In practice the rider will need to attend to longitudinal flexion, impulsion, rhythm and so forth, at the same time. Here, however, such considerations are set aside so as to be able to concentrate on the aids that are directly responsible for indicating the bend and the direction of movement.

Bending

At times when lateral bending is not required, such as when halting or when walking or trotting on straight lines, the rider must sit with his body facing directly forwards, keeping his shoulders parallel to those of the horse. His legs must be held neither one more advanced than the other, in a position just behind the girth.

When working at canter, when riding at any gait on a circular track, or when moving laterally the horse must show some degree of lateral bending. To help him to bend the rider must modify his own position

Incorrect

Bending.

in the saddle. The rider must slide back the leg on the outside of the bend so that the heel lies further back than the heel of the inside leg. The actual amount of movement will depend on the degree of bending required, but will usually be around four inches. It is important when moving the leg back to take the knee and thigh back a little and not merely to bend at the knee. The latter action is a much less effective aid which will cause the rider's outside heel to rise and will prevent the horse from being given the extra assistance of a change in weight distribution.

The rider must turn his upper body to keep his shoulders in parallel with those of the laterally bent horse, by moving the shoulder on the outside of the bend forward. This new position of the shoulders combined with the offset position of the legs, slightly changes the distribution of weight in the saddle by shifting it to the inside. This in turn encourages the horse to engage his inside hind leg, which completes the bending.

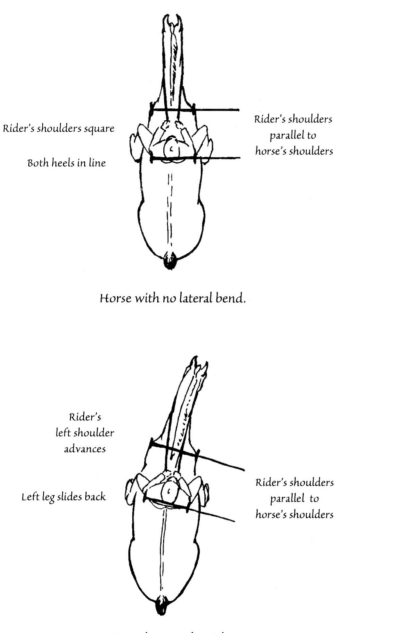

Rider's shoulders square

Both heels in line

Rider's shoulders
parallel to
horse's shoulders

Horse with no lateral bend.

Rider's
left shoulder
advances

Left leg slides back

Rider's shoulders
parallel to
horse's shoulders

Horse bent to the right.

On a trained horse no direct action will be required from the hands when applying the aids; the correct action will automatically come about as a result of repositioning the shoulders. As the horse engages his inside hind leg he will lighten the contact on the inside rein. With the less advanced horse it may be necessary to lead him into the bend with the inside rein and yield the outside rein to allow him to stretch. The rider who is uncertain what to do will need the assistance of a knowledgeable teacher.

Lateral Exercises

In all lateral work the horse must be bent, and so without exception the rider's position must be modified to help the horse to assume the required bending. From this curved position, if the aids for the lateral exercises are not applied the horse will naturally progress on a circular track, the size of the circle being dependent upon the degree of bending obtained. If this turns out not to be the case then the rider's position is at fault, and it must be adjusted until the required effect is obtained.

The aids for causing the various lateral movements can conveniently be considered as ways of preventing the horse from continuing on his preferred circular track and allowing the required lateral movement as the only possible escape route.

When applying aids for the lateral movements the seat must always be kept still; there must never be any pushing or shoving.

Shoulder-in

For a right shoulder-in the horse must be bent to the right. The rider must press his right leg down into the stirrup and into the horse's side, and keep a contact on the left rein to prevent the horse moving directly forwards onto a circular track. The contact on the right rein must remain light so as not to interfere with the movement of the right shoulder or the engagement of the right hind leg.

The influence of the rider's weight through the inside of his seat,

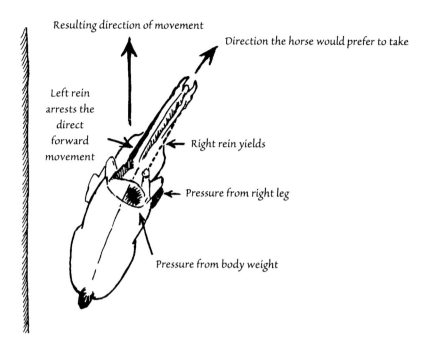

Resulting direction of movement

Direction the horse would prefer to take

Left rein
arrests the
direct
forward
movement

Right rein yields

Pressure from right leg

Pressure from body weight

Aiding the right shoulder-in.

combined with the pressure from the inside leg guides the horse in the required direction.

Aids for a right shoulder-out are identical. The only difference is that the exercise is practised with the wall to the right instead of to the left.

Haunches-in

For haunches-in to the left, the horse must be bent to the left. The rider's right leg presses against the horse's side to encourage him to step sideways with his right hind leg. The rider's weight acts downwards through the inside of his seat in such a way that the horse will move towards the left in order to keep the rider properly balanced on his back. The rider's leg and shoulder positioning will be sufficient to achieve this effect, and the rider must take care not to lean sideways.

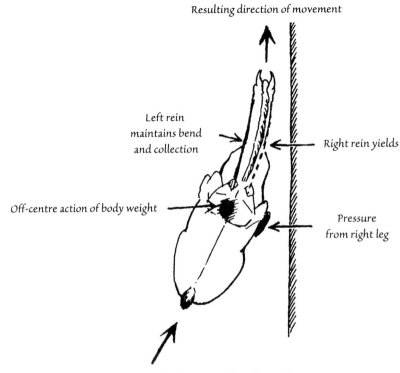

Resulting direction of movement

Left rein
maintains bend
and collection

Right rein yields

Off-centre action of body weight

Pressure
from right leg

Direction the horse would prefer to take

Aiding the haunches-in left with the less experienced horse.

On an advanced horse, where the rider's inside leg is effective in bringing about good engagement of the horse's inside hind leg, it will be possible to lighten the contact on the inside rein. In the early stages, however, it will be necessary to lighten the outside rein, otherwise the horse will have difficulty in maintaining the bend and the collection, and his outside foreleg will be restricted in its movement. The aids for haunches-in on the less experienced horse are depicted in the illustration.

For haunches-out to the left the aids are identical. The only difference is that the wall is to the left of the horse instead of to the right.

Half-Pass

Because the half-pass is a very similar movement to the haunches-in the aids for producing it are also similar. At half-pass the outside foreleg is required to cross over in front of the inside foreleg. Consequently it is particularly important with the less advanced horse to yield the outside rein to give freedom of movement to his outside shoulder.

For a right half-pass the horse must be bent to the right. The rider's left leg will assist the crossing of the horse's left hind leg, and the influence of his weight will encourage the horse to travel forwards and sideways towards the right to keep the rider in balance.

Here is another case where the aids evolve and become more refined as

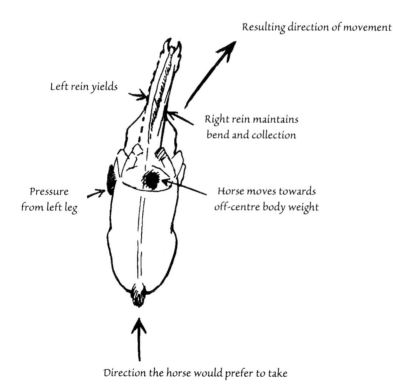

Aiding the right half-pass with the less experienced horse.

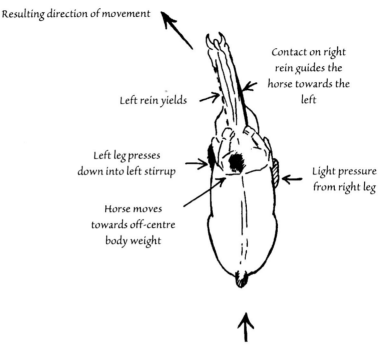

Resulting direction of movement

Contact on right rein guides the horse towards the left

Left rein yields

Left leg presses down into left stirrup

Light pressure from right leg

Horse moves towards off-centre body weight

Direction the horse would prefer to take

Aiding the left half-pass with the advanced horse.

the training progresses. As with the haunches-in it would be possible to yield the inside rein when working an experienced school horse, provided that the rider's inside leg is effective in engaging the horse's inside hind leg. Yielding the inside rein when riding a novice, however, is likely to result in losing the bend and the collection. The aids must be adjusted according to necessities of the moment.

As the horse becomes more experienced the rider will find that he need not make so much use of his outside leg. The horse will begin to respond more to the influence of the weight aids as the rider presses more firmly on the inside stirrup. The yielding inside rein will further assist the engagement of the inside hind leg, whilst the resultant contact on the outside rein will help to direct the horse diagonally forwards and sideways.

CHAPTER SEVEN

Flying Changes

The flying change of lead allows the rider to change direction at canter without having to change down to another pace and strike off again. The horse performs flying changes naturally, so they fall within the realms of classical riding.

Multiple flying changes executed in quick succession are not so natural to the horse, and their practice in classical riding has been the subject of some controversy in the past. These changes were unknown to the eighteenth-century riding masters. The flying change at every stride was first demonstrated by the nineteenth-century Frenchman Baucher. Much of his work was controversial, and in Vienna he was referred to as 'the grave-digger of French equitation'. Nevertheless, it is interesting to note that although it bases its training largely on the teachings of La Guérinière, the Spanish Riding School does also include these multiple changes in its performances!

Flying changes contribute very little to the overall development of the horse as they do nothing to aid collection. They are usually taught at the collected canter where the rider has greater control, but the horse can perform them quite easily at the extended canter too.

With regard to multiple changes, although they might be of dubious merit, practised in moderation they are certainly not harmful, and there is no reason why the horse should not learn to do them. Indeed one benefit is that they can help to make him more agile. They are also a good test of riding ability as they rank among the more difficult feats of horsemanship.

Teaching the Flying Change

Before the horse can be expected to perform the flying change his canter should be well balanced, and he should be adept at simple changes - i.e. canter to walk and walk to canter transitions. He must also be able to move easily in counter-canter.

The aids for the flying change are similar to those for any strike-off into canter, but the change must be signalled mainly by the rider's new outside leg. This leg should contact the horse behind the girth. The new inside leg should be passive - it can even be taken away from the horse's side to avoid any confusion. The new inside rein should be yielded to allow the horse's inside shoulder to move forwards.

The timing of the aids is important or problems will arise later on when teaching two-time and one-time changes. The rider's new outside leg should contact the horse as the diagonal of the last canter stride on the old lead impacts with the ground. If the aids are delayed much more than this the horse will have to put in an extra stride before he can change.

There are several ways in which the flying change can be taught. With a well-balanced horse it may be sufficient to ride a change of direction at canter and to ask for a flying change of lead as the direction is changed. This could be done, for example, by changing rein across the diagonal and attempting a flying change at the end of the diagonal; or it could be done at the cross-over point of a figure-of-eight. It is very important that the horse is not allowed to throw his shoulder into the new direction.

These methods will not work for all horses. Some will need more help. Baucher's technique was to prepare the horse by riding a canter to halt transition and to follow this immediately by riding a halt to canter onto the opposite lead. When the horse could master this, Baucher proceeded to omit the halt and ask for a flying change of lead directly. This method has the advantage that the rider is in greater control of the horse's balance; but the disadvantage is that it can produce rather stilted changes that do not flow forwards very smoothly.

A better approach is derived from the simple change of lead. Canter to walk and walk to canter transitions can be made to flow more easily than canter to halt and halt to canter transitions, and a better flying change is likely to result. A very effective procedure is outlined below:

♦ Work on a large circle to the right.

♦ Pinpoint a certain spot where you wish to attempt the flying change.

♦ Put the horse in a left lead counter-canter.

♦ At the chosen spot ride a simple change, passing directly to walk, and calling out 'canter' as you ask for the strike-off from walk into a right lead canter.

♦ Repeat the procedure a few times trying to reduce the number of walk steps to a minimum.

♦ On the next occasion do not ask for the counter-canter to walk transition, but on reaching the chosen spot in counter-canter give the aids for a right lead canter directly, and call out 'canter'.

♦ If nothing happens try again, but usually the horse will try something, even if he doesn't succeed in producing a good flying change.

♦ Any positive response should be rewarded, and the exercise should not be attempted again until the next day.

If the horse is first taught the left-to-right flying change, then this should be mastered before any attempt is made at the right-to-left change. When the latter change is taught the same procedure should be adopted, working on a large circle to the left. The fact that the horse can change from left to right will not make it any easier for him to change from right to left, so just as much time and patience will be required as before.

The rider should always ensure that the rhythm does not alter. The horse may try to speed up after the change, and this must be prevented.

This picture shows the right moment to ask for a left to right flying change. The rider applies his left leg behind the girth as the left hind leg and right foreleg are grounded.
(Photo: John Birt)

When counter-canter to true canter flying changes have been mastered the horse will be ready to try true canter to true canter flying changes through a change of direction. After that he should be taught to execute them on straight lines.

As a test of his obedience the horse should then be asked to perform true canter to counter-canter changes on large circles in both directions. He can be considered to have mastered single flying changes when he can perform a figure-of-eight in either direction in counter-canter with a flying change from counter-canter to counter-canter at the cross-over point.

Teaching Multiple Flying Changes

Before multiple flying changes can be attempted the horse must have mastered single changes.

First, determine the smallest number of canter strides that the horse can do after striking off into canter and before returning to a walk or a halt. This is a good guide to the smallest number of canter strides that he will be capable of doing between flying changes. If the number is more than about six, then he is not yet ready for multiple changes. For the first attempt at multiple changes the number should be exceeded by one or two strides.

At first the changes should be practised on a straight line. Whenever a smaller number of strides between changes is being attempted for the first time it is important to ask for only two flying changes. The number of changes can be increased gradually as the horse becomes more proficient.

The number of strides between changes should never be decreased until the horse has thoroughly mastered a string of changes at the previous number of strides, preferably on a large circle as well as on a straight line. The number should only be decreased by one.

When attempting a smaller number of strides, the flying changes can either be placed within a long stretch of canter, or they can be placed at the end of a string of changes of one or two more strides per change than the number being attempted. In the latter case they should be followed by a stretch of canter with no changes. For example, to start one-time changes ride:

... left · left · left · **left** · **right** · **left** · left · left · left ...

or

... left · left · right · right · left · **left** · **right** · **left** · left · left · left ...

If the horse starts anticipating changes, then the rider should return to long stretches of change-free canter, or to multiple changes with more strides per change, before making another attempt.

CHAPTER EIGHT

Extremes of Collection

The limits of collection are represented at trot by the piaffe and at canter by the pirouette. Both exercises are good for the horse because they help to strengthen his back and hindquarters. Related to the piaffe is the passage - an elevated floating trot.

These exercises should not be attempted until the horse has been thoroughly prepared by means of a systematic schooling programme which has been designed to strengthen the relevant muscles and lower the haunches by means of easier exercises. The horse must be able to work easily at the school trot and the school canter, that is with more weight on the haunches than is usually demanded at the collected trot and canter.

All the earlier training of the horse should contribute something to the bending of the joints of the hind legs and the lowering of the haunches. Some of the more effective exercises are turns on the haunches, haunches-in on a circle, canter to halt and halt to canter transitions. Also the canter pirouette will help to prepare the horse for piaffe, and vice versa.

This level of collection may be beyond the scope of some horses, and it will be beyond the ability of some riders too. Nevertheless the exercises are easy to ride if the horse is properly prepared.

Provided that the horse executes the movements correctly, the ability to train him to this level is proof that the principles of classical training have been understood and put into practice. The converse may also be true: failure to train a suitable horse to this level can indicate that the rider has not understood the essence of classical riding. In all probability the horse has not fully mastered his earlier lessons and the rider is unaware of this. The rider who cannot imagine how a piaffe might be ridden has not understood how to ride the horse in collection.

No far-reaching conclusions can be drawn about the abilities of the rider who succeeds in obtaining a piaffe or a canter pirouette on a horse trained by someone else. This is merely a question of correct application of the aids rather than a thorough mastery of the art of riding, and consequently it cannot be considered a great achievement.

Teaching the Piaffe and the Passage

The Piaffe

The piaffe is a highly collected trot executed on the spot. It represents the ultimate in collection at trot, and is one of the most difficult exercises to master. Even in international competition it is rare to see a good piaffe. The best place to see the piaffe is undoubtedly at the Spanish Riding School in Vienna, where standards are set that few can hope to reach. There are in addition a few masters who can perform the exercise well - the late Nuno Oliveira had exceptional abilities and he could keep his horses in piaffe for some five or ten minutes.

Those people who do not ride piaffe themselves may be tempted to think that the horse must be forced to perform in this way. This is absolutely not the case. The piaffe is a natural movement that is well within the capabilities of the properly prepared horse.

Direct upward transitions and extensions will be much improved if they are ridden directly following an attempt at piaffe. The piaffe is also the foundation upon which schools above the ground are built.

The piaffe should be taught before the passage otherwise it may never be obtainable; the horse will use the passage as an evasion and will be able to avoid performing the piaffe. Occasionally a horse will offer the piaffe as an evasion. This horse is the exception to the rule, and he should be taught the passage first.

With the piaffe, as with any other sort of trot, there must be a moment of suspension; but this moment can be so short as to be imperceptible. There is a difference between a trot in which the period of suspension is reduced to nothing, and an alternate raising and grounding of diagonals - the latter would not qualify as a piaffe. Some horses will offer a piaffe with more pronounced suspension, and this will look more impressive.

In order to be able to thrust himself upwards and produce a period of suspension without gaining ground to the front, the horse must bend the joints of his hind legs, tilt his pelvis, and lower his haunches. The horse is not ready to learn the piaffe until he has been made sufficiently strong by means of easier exercises which demand a lowering of the haunches but to a lesser degree. The rider who goes through the motions of these exercises without getting the horse a little more onto his haunches will fail in his attempts at piaffe.

The nervous, excited horse will not show a proper piaffe because he will squander his energies. A dull, listless horse will never be coaxed into piaffe either. For a good piaffe the horse needs controlled strength and power rather than nervous energy. He should show mature calmness and equanimity, but he needs enough adrenalin flowing to make him feel animated.

Some authors imply that to ride a piaffe the rider has to contain the horse's desire to move forwards. Strictly speaking this is true, for unless the horse is eager to gain ground, the rider will be unable to obtain the piaffe. Nevertheless it can also be misleading, and it would

At piaffe the horse must lower his haunches, engage his hind legs, and spring from resilient hocks.

be very wrong to suggest that the rider must struggle to hold the horse back. The aids should be very light, and it is certainly not a question of driving hard and holding hard. The best piaffes are executed on slack reins.

Every type of trot has a forward component and an upward component. When asking for a piaffe the rider must know how to engage and lower the haunches so he can obtain only the upward component. Any unwanted forward component should not be asked for in the first place.

When applying the aids, the rider can try applying his legs a little further back than usual, and he can raise his hands a little. He can also experiment with changing his seat either more onto the crotch or more onto the seat bones.

The horse should move so softly that very little of the impact with the ground is felt by the rider. What impact there is must be absorbed by the rider's lower back and must not be felt as a pressure variation between the seat and the saddle, as this would impede the piaffe, which is difficult enough to obtain even with a good seat.

There are several methods that can be tried when teaching the piaffe. It

Some horses may try to trot on the spot by springing from the fetlocks. They take the weight back by raising the head instead of lowering the haunches. This is not a piaffe and must not be allowed.

can be approached from a collected trot, from a collected walk, or from a halt. It can be taught in hand, or ridden, with or without the assistance of a trainer on the ground.

One very useful method is to practise a series of trot to halt and halt to trot transitions. The frequency of the transitions should gradually be increased, and the rider should ask for more collection and less ground coverage each time he asks for a trot.

Another effective approach is to ride a collected walk interspersed with the occasional attempt at piaffe, asking for a very collected trot with very little ground coverage. The collected walk can be interrupted by turns on the haunches to increase the bending of the joints of the hind legs.

When approaching the piaffe from a collected trot the rider practises lengthening and shortening strides - lengthening up to a collected trot, and shortening down to piaffe. The collected trot can include periods of haunches-in on a circle to encourage the bending of the joints of the hind legs. Collected trot to walk transitions should also be practised as this will discourage the horse from starting to anticipate the piaffe.

Nicole Uphoff applies her lower leg a little further back than usual when riding a piaffe. Notice her light rein contact and Rembrandt's relaxed expression.
(Photo: Werner Ernst)

The rider may find it easier to keep the horse straight if he carries two schooling whips. Light touches on the top of the croup with the whip may help to produce a piaffe.

If the rider has the assistance of a trainer on the ground, the latter can touch the hind cannons of the horse at the correct moments to help with the exercise. However, there is always the danger that the horse will only perform a piaffe when the trainer is present, so this method should not be over-used.

Teaching the piaffe in hand looks very easy when done by an expert, but in reality it is very difficult. Nevertheless it is easier for the horse to do a piaffe without the weight of a rider on his back, and so the method is invaluable to those who can master it. The horse must be used to working in hand with side-reins and cavesson. He must be able to halt, walk on, rein-back and trot, and he must lift his hind legs when the trainer touches them with the whip. The difficulty is in knowing exactly where to touch and at which instant. There is also some danger involved as the horse may kick out or make sudden leaps to release the tension in his hind limbs.

Once the horse begins to be able to piaffe it is important that he is allowed to stop before he is so tired that the exercise collapses. In this way he will not find the piaffe distasteful, and he will gradually be able to do more steps.

The Passage

When the horse can sustain about six steps of piaffe, work at passage can commence. The passage is an elevated floating trot with a prolonged period of suspension, in which the horse appears to move in slow motion. It requires almost as much collection as the piaffe, combined with tremendous power in the hindquarters. The horse must stay well rounded with lowered haunches so that he appears to move uphill. His back must not hollow or his hind legs will splay out behind.

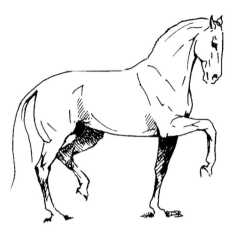

At passage the horse should engage his hind legs and give the appearance of moving uphill.

One easy way to produce the passage is to allow the horse forwards after executing two or three steps of piaffe. Alternatively it can be started from a collected walk or trot by giving similar aids to those for the piaffe but allowing the horse to gain ground straight away. If the horse is being taught the passage by allowing him to move forwards from a piaffe, the rider must also spend some time practising piaffe to trot transitions, otherwise the horse may develop the habit of moving off into passage.

The passage is easier for the horse to sustain than the piaffe, but nevertheless the demands should be increased only gradually. The passage will strengthen the haunches so that the piaffe will then show some improvement. Another way of encouraging the horse to sustain the piaffe is to allow one or two steps of passage after every few steps of piaffe. This relieves the tension in the muscles before the piaffe is restarted.

Every step of the passage has to be controlled to maintain the proper degree of collection, suspension and forward progression. If the horse is allowed to gain too much ground then the movement will have the character of an extended trot rather than a passage. The rider should bring the horse back to a trot before the passage deteriorates. With practice the horse will be able to sustain the passage for longer periods .

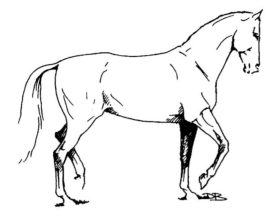

Dressage competitors usually show a flatter passage which lacks engagement. This falls short of the classical ideal.

Obviously the passage is not only ridden on straight lines, and the rider may wish to move off from piaffe into a passage on a circle either to the right or to the left. This adds another complication to the piaffe, which must be practised with either a right bend or a left bend so that the transition into the passage on the circle will flow smoothly.

At this point the rider will probably find that one piaffe is easier to ride than the other; in other words the horse has still not been properly straightened. A return to earlier work will be necessary to improve the situation. It is also possible to practise lateral work at the passage, and consequently some extra exercises become available to the rider at this stage of training.

Teaching the Canter Pirouette

In classical riding the pirouette marks the limit of collection at canter. In fact the horse is capable of cantering on the spot, and this requires even more collection, but since this movement is not volunteered in nature it is considered out of bounds in contemporary classical circles.

When the horse executes a canter pirouette, each stride must be a proper three-beat canter stride, and the rhythm should be exactly the

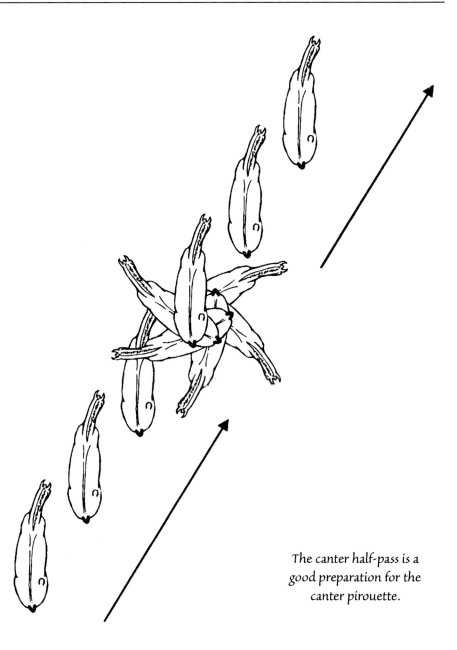

The canter half-pass is a good preparation for the canter pirouette.

same as the canter which preceded it. The inside hind foot marks the centre of the pirouette, but this foot must be raised and lowered as is normal in a canter; it must not remain fixed on the ground.

It is not a pirouette if the horse throws himself round without carrying and controlling his weight on lowered haunches. Such a movement is

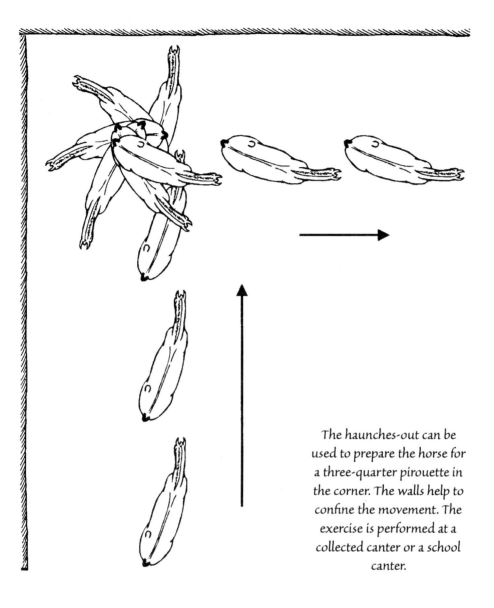

The haunches-out can be used to prepare the horse for a three-quarter pirouette in the corner. The walls help to confine the movement. The exercise is performed at a collected canter or a school canter.

known as a 'tornado', and again is outside the bounds of classical riding. The horse must remain upright; he is not allowed to lean inwards and give the appearance of falling round.

The pirouette should be ridden as a canter half-pass on a very small circle whose radius is almost nothing. The horse must be on a tangent to the circle so that at each stride the inside hind foot has to step forwards to reach the next point on the circumference. If the rider attempts to ride the pirouette as a full pass on a circle then the centre of the circle will be directly behind the inside hind foot, and this foot will have to step sideways to reach the next place on the ground. In attempting this the canter is likely to fall apart and become a 'terre-à-terre' - a series of leaps where the two fore feet move together followed by the two hind feet. This movement is another that is now out of bounds in classical riding, because it is artificial: the horse does not display it in nature.

Within the limits of the horse's capability the rider must be able to dictate the exact number of canter strides that make up the complete pirouette. Usually six to eight strides is reasonable.

Just as the piaffe feels different from the collected trot, so too should the canter at the pirouette feel different from the collected canter. The difference in feeling arises because of the increased collection required. A correct pirouette cannot be ridden by turning the horse around the haunches at a collected canter, the collection must be deliberately increased further so that the horse can support more of his body weight on lowered haunches. Before attempting a pirouette the horse must have mastered the school canter, and the rider must be certain that he can control the tempo at the haunches-out and at the half-pass so that it remains slow and measured.

One might expect that by riding haunches-in on a circle and gradually diminishing the radius the end result would be a pirouette. With this approach, however, it is very difficult for the rider to control the engagement of the inside hind leg, which tends to step out sideways instead of directly forwards and underneath the weight. Nevertheless voltes ridden at haunches-in are a good preparation.

One good method is to start from a haunches-out position and to attempt a three-quarter pirouette when reaching the corner of the arena. For example, ride a little way in from the long side of the arena and parallel to it, with the wall on the left. Strike off into left lead counter-canter and move the horse into a haunches-out position. On reaching the corner attempt a threequarter pirouette to the left. The two walls of the arena will be found to be a great help. Continue in

Monica Theodorescu is riding Ganimedes in a canter pirouette to the left. She has increased his collection by lowering his haunches. *(Photo: Wener Ernst)*

haunches-out parallel to the short side of the arena.

Another excellent approach is to ride a few canter voltes on light reins, followed by a canter to walk transition. This should be followed immediately by a turn or two on the forehand, the horse moving away from the inside leg. The rider should then ask for another transition into canter and immediately attempt a pirouette or part thereof, using an extremely light rein contact.

The pirouette, or part thereof, can also be attempted from a canter half-pass, as this will give the horse good engagement and bend to the inside.

When the pirouette has been perfected the horse will show less lateral bending than he does at half-pass, but when teaching the pirouette the rider should ask for rather more bending as otherwise the horse will be liable to counter-flex, and disengage his inside hind leg.

The rider should pinpoint a spot on the ground to use as the centre of the pirouette and keep his eye on it so he can check how well the exercise is performed.

CHAPTER NINE

Training Procedure

T his chapter is a very brief guide to the procedures which should be adopted when training the horse on classical lines. It gives an idea of the order in which new exercises can be introduced to the horse, without elaborating on the complexities of how the results might be achieved. In practice each horse must be treated as an individual, and it is not really appropriate to stick to a rigid timetable. Nevertheless the schedule outlined here is a reasonable working plan and is intended to be particularly useful to those having only a limited experience of training horses. The whole range of training from unbroken youngster to Grand Prix dressage horse is covered.

It is traditional to warn that schooling the horse is a long, painstaking process; certainly no short cuts should be made, and every horse should be given a thorough education. On the other hand, there are plenty of cases where schooling progresses far too slowly. Consequently there are some riders who should be encouraged to accelerate their training programme if they hope to produce a reasonable riding horse before he is too old to be ridden any more!

First some early preparations for the young horse are explained. For the actual training it is best to wait until the horse is approaching four years of age, because the younger horse will not be sufficiently mature to cope with the demands. A four-year training programme is then presented, and it starts with lungeing. An experienced trainer may be able to complete the job in three years, but others may take longer than four. The programme can be lengthened or shortened as required.

Early Preparations

A number of preparations can be made before the horse's training begins. They will help to ease the potentially traumatic transition from the freedom of the paddock to the confines of the stable and the riding school. The horse should become accustomed to being handled and he can be introduced to some of the equipment that the trainer will be using. Great care must be taken in these early stages not to frighten the horse. He must be handled firmly but gently.

First of all fit the young horse with a headcollar and lead him about in hand. Lead him from either side, and teach him to stand still and to walk on. A hand can be used on his side in the place where the rider's leg will one day be applied, and much use should be made of the voice. Pat the horse or give him tit-bits when he is good, but do not punish him for not responding.

A roller will eventually be required when lungeing, but there is no reason why the horse should not get used to wearing one beforehand. When fitting a roller for the first time it is wise to proceed cautiously because the horse may panic and react violently. Do not buckle the roller up straight away but hold it in place so that it can be removed easily in case of emergency. Reassure the horse until he accepts the strange feeling calmly. For the sake of safety it is better not to work in a confined space.

The lungeing cavesson can also be fitted before it is needed, and it can be used for leading the horse about. Again he should be led from both sides. Protective boots can be fitted too, as this will save time when the lunge training starts. It takes most horses a little while to get used to wearing something strange on their legs and they often do not walk normally at first.

Particular care must be taken when fitting the bit. It is vital that it fits the horse's mouth properly in terms of width, thickness and shape, so that he can carry it comfortably. Thicker bits are milder but there must be room for him to close his mouth easily. A snaffle should be used in preference to a special bit with keys, because the objective is to encourage the horse to carry the bit in a still, quiet mouth. The bit should removed fairly soon on the first occasion, perhaps after about half a minute. Each day it can be fitted again and left in for a little longer. In this way the horse will gradually get accustomed to carrying it.

Always lead the horse from a headcollar or a cavesson rather than from the bit, or there could be problems in establishing a proper contact when training begins. At this stage the bit is merely something for the horse to carry.

Lungeing + Longreining

♦ First check that the horse is used to all the equipment. Fit the lunge rein to the centre ring of the cavesson and check that he leads from either side. It is a good idea to stroke him with the lungeing whip to ensure that he is not frightened of it. Although it is called a whip the horse is never whipped with it; it merely serves as an extension of the trainer's arm so he can work at a convenient distance from the horse.

♦ At the start of the lunge training the sessions should last only a few minutes. The horse should not be over-worked, but provided the work is methodical he will get stronger by degrees and the time can gradually be extended to some twenty or thirty minutes. It should be possible to work him a little every day. When all goes well a shorter session will be appropriate. Always end on a good note.

♦ Lengthen the lunge rein a little and walk the horse in large circles on both reins. Practise getting him to stand still and to walk on.

♦ If the horse tries to cut in then point the lunge whip towards his shoulder. If he succeeds in cutting in just take him back to the circle and start again, but do not punish him. Although there must be some limit to misbehaviour, generally when the horse plays up it is best to stop and start again without reacting to it. If he gets too boisterous the lunge rein can be tugged to keep him in check.

♦ Fasten side-reins to the bit. They should both be the same length and quite long, or the horse might rear up and go over backwards. He should just be able to take up the slack in the reins when he stretches his neck forwards. Side-reins will teach him to seek a proper contact with the bit.

♦ Side-reins will also help to prevent some of the wayward behaviour that the horse may think of when the trainer is not right beside him to keep him in check. The trainer will always have more control when he is close to the horse, so it is better in the early days to walk

The Spanish Riding School of Vienna displays some of its advanced stallions in long reins. The trainer is able to continue walking regardless of whether the horse walks, trots or canters. To enable this, the ridden training must be so thorough that the horse can easily maintain a slow school trot or school canter. (*Photo: Andreas Jarc*)

around on a circle inside the one the horse is working on. Later on the trainer can stand at the centre.

♦ Keep the horse on a large circle and start work at trot. It is very important not to work on small circles as this would put too much strain on his joints. Practise walk to trot and trot to walk transitions.

♦ Make sure the horse steps forward well with his hind feet. They should reach the footprints made by his fore feet. Make sure he bends his body in the direction of the circle, and ensure that he stretches forward and downwards to seek a contact with the bit. If these points are not attended to the lungeing will be a waste of time.

♦ As each session progresses the side-reins can gradually be shortened. As the training progresses they can start at a shorter length. They must never be used to hold the horse's head in position. They should be shortened to take up the slack that arises because the horse is becoming more collected.

♦ Practise lengthening and shortening the strides at trot.

♦ Start work at canter. Attend to the relaxation and the lateral bending. Practise transitions to and from trot, and practise lengthening and shortening the strides.

♦ Saddle the horse and repeat the previous work with the stirrups run up and held in place so they cannot slide down. Afterwards lower the stirrups and work the horse carefully to get him used to the feeling of the stirrups moving about against his sides.

♦ At this stage in the horse's education he can be backed. This should be done cautiously by degrees so as not to frighten him and cause an accident. The trainer should hold the horse while an assistant leans across his back. The horse should be reassured. No further progress should be made until the horse accepts the weight calmly. Great care must be taken when sitting upright on the horse's back because the unaccustomed sight of a rider in this position can startle the horse and cause him to panic.

♦ If the horse seems safe enough on the lunge then repeat all the previous work with a rider mounted. At first the rider must just be a passenger and not contribute to the aids. Later the rider can apply aids together with the trainer, and finally the trainer can allow the rider's aids to dominate.

♦ The period of lunge training should last about three months. If the horse is worked on fewer than about four days a week then the training period will have to be extended. If the horse is making good progress, two months may be adequate. The longer this phase of training lasts the easier the initial ridden training will be.

Initial Ridden Training

♦ Walk out in the company of a sensible horse, and preferably a sensible rider - someone who has ridden young horses will be more considerate. Don't get the horse excited. Avoid narrow tracks and any possible hazards. Start with very short sessions. Gradually increase the time.

♦ Rest the hands on the saddle arch or the thighs so that the contact with the bit feels the same to the horse as it did when the side-reins were attached on the lunge. Use the voice as an aid. Sit upright but be ready to lean back if the horse bucks.

♦ Introduce short periods of trot, making sure you can get back to a walk.

♦ Introduce short periods of canter.

♦ Gradually increase the work over about three months to get the horse fit enough to start some ridden school work. For variety, some days ride the horse, and some days lunge him.

♦ The first year's training is completed with the next phase of ridden school work lasting about six months. This can start at one or two days a week and build up to about four days a week. The objective is to render the horse active, calm, and straight, and to show the beginnings of collection while riding simple patterns and transitions.

♦ The work to be covered in the initial schooling is as follows:

- Collection at trot.

- Turning in away from the wall at the start of a long side and returning to it before the end of the same side.

- Large circles at trot.

- Definite trot to walk transitions.

- Trot to canter transitions.

- Collection at canter.

- Large circles at canter.

- Spirals at trot.

- Small circles at trot.

- Serpentines at trot.

- Figures-of-eight at trot.

- Halts of increasing duration, keeping the horse still. He need not be square.

- A little medium walk, and plenty of free walk on a long rein.

- Lengthening and shortening strides at trot.

- Spirals at canter.

- Small circles at canter.

- Lengthening and shortening strides at canter.

- Turns on the forehand.

Schooling in the Second Year

♦ The number of schooling sessions per week can be increased. Four to six sessions of about thirty minutes is a good guideline.

♦ Some work in hand should continue. On the lunge more collection at trot and canter are the main objectives. It is also a good idea to teach the horse to stand square at the halt and to rein back in hand. For these exercises stand by the horse's shoulder and lead him alongside a wall or rail with a short rein attached to the central ring of the cavesson.

If, when halting, the horse trails a hind leg, encourage him to move it forwards by tapping it gently with the lungeing whip on the cannon or fetlock. Similarly if he takes all his weight on one hind leg and rests the other, tap the weighted leg and he will shift his weight onto the other one.

To teach the rein-back, make gentle backward actions with the lunge rein, and if necessary tap the horse on the chest. Always walk him forwards again after he has taken a few steps backwards.

♦ A little jumping will do no harm.

♦ New work to be covered in the schooling is as follows:

- Shoulder-in at walk.

- Shoulder-in at trot.

- Haunches-in at walk.

- Haunches-in at trot.

- Haunches-in and haunches-out on the circle at trot.

- Half-pass at walk.

- Half-pass at trot.

- Full pass at walk.

- The horse can be introduced to spurs at this stage.

- Trot to halt transitions.

- Halt to trot transitions.

- Square halts.

- Plié canters.

- Walk to canter transitions.

- Canter to walk transitions.

- Halt to canter transitions.

- Canter to halt transitions.

Schooling in the Third Year

♦ There will be many times when earlier work must be reviewed.

♦ New work to be covered in the schooling is as follows:

- Extended walk.

- Collected walk.

- Transitions between collected and extended walk.

- Turn on the haunches.

- Rein-back.

- Halt to rein-back transitions.

- Rein-back to walk transitions.

- Walk to rein-back transitions with the intermediate halt reduced to a minimum.

- Rein-back to trot transitions.

- Rein-back to canter transitions.

- Counter-canter.

- Trot to counter-canter.

- Walk to counter-canter.

- Counter-canter to walk.

- Flying change from counter-canter to true canter.

- Flying change from true canter to true canter through a change of direction.

- Flying change from true canter to true canter on a straight line.

- Flying change from true canter to counter-canter.

- Half-pass at canter.

The horse's basic training is now complete, and he should be a good riding horse. All riding horses should be put through the above training programme. Further schooling can be regarded as specialised dressage work. If no more schooling is to be done the horse can be introduced to the double bridle, but this should not be used when teaching new exercises. Dressage horses should be kept in a snaffle until their education is complete at the end of the next phase.

Schooling in the Fourth and Subsequent Years

♦ In-hand work can include working towards piaffe – getting the horse to raise his back a little and lower his haunches, working on a very collected trot.

♦ At this stage much time will be spent reviewing earlier work and establishing the basic requirements of moving with activity, calmness and straightness.

♦ New work to be introduced is shown overleaf:

- Counter change of hand in half-pass at trot.

- Counter change of hand in half-pass at canter.

- Haunches-out along the wall at canter. (Counter-canter with the tail to the wall.)

- Haunches-in on the circle at canter.

- Haunches-out on the circle at (counter-) canter.

- Passade at canter.

- Canter pirouettes.

- Extended trot to halt transitions.

- Extended canter to halt transitions.

- Halt to extended trot transitions.

- Halt to extended canter transitions.

- Flying changes after a given number of strides.

- Piaffe.

- Passage.

- Transitions between piaffe and trot.

- Transitions between passage and trot.

- Transitions between piaffe and passage.

The horse should now be at Grand Prix level. Horses showing superior strength, collection and talent may be able to proceed to schools above the ground.

CHAPTER TEN

Remedial Schooling

Training the horse would be a simple matter if it were merely a question of following a pre-determined sequence of exercises. In reality the path is strewn with obstacles, and most horses experience some difficulties with their work. It is worth bearing in mind that all schooling should be considered to be remedial: the rider detects a problem and then applies those exercises that are most likely to help the horse to overcome it.

Horses come from a variety of different backgrounds, and they vary tremendously in their training needs. Some horses are more difficult to train than others, but the classical system can and should be applied to them all. With those that have been started properly the future training should be reasonably straightforward. Where the horse's education has been neglected, remarkable progress can often be made once a proper schooling programme is resumed. More skill, experience and patience will be needed when dealing with the more difficult cases, but every step in the right direction will make all the time and effort worthwhile.

Because young horses can be difficult to handle, most people buy ready made horses rather than unbroken youngsters. Not everyone wants to master the first stages of educating a horse, and by buying an older animal who has already had some training the rider can avoid the youthful excesses to which the younger horse is prone, and can enjoy a reasonable ride straight away. There can, however, also be problems when training older horses, and overcoming these difficulties can sometimes be harder than learning to cope with young horses.

Experience shows that it is easier to train an unbroken horse than it is to retrain a horse who has been started incorrectly. The latter will require a great deal of corrective work before any further progress can be considered. Such a horse will need plenty of time to learn the basics of moving actively forwards in a relaxed manner, on the aids and straight.

Some horses come from other branches of riding, such as racing, for example, where the early training is different. They might perhaps have developed the habit of cantering on one lead only. Here much of the remedial work would involve straightening the horse. Some horses will have been ridden badly in the past. They may have had to contend with strong pressure on the bit. They may have been above the bit for months or perhaps even years, or they may never have been straightened. There are many possibilities. Usually there are no insurmountable problems, but the schooling will take a little longer than usual, and more patience will be required.

Because horses are such creatures of habit they tend to get set in their ways, and when the rider asks for something different they can be extremely clever at evading the aids and resisting any change. The rider will need to find ways around this. There is a danger here that riders who are lacking in knowledge and experience may be tempted to punish their horses, when in fact they might be better employed in seeking to improve their own riding skills. One of the reasons for schooling is to make life easier for the horse, and care must be taken that this object is not defeated. Sometimes it is better to be less demanding so that the horse can be rewarded as soon as he starts to show willing.

Successful training must of course be based on a system of reward and punishment because the horse has to have some means of distinguishing right from wrong. The word *punishment*, however, is perhaps an unfortunate one, because it conjures up pictures of violent assaults upon the horse. Every horse must respect his rider, but in the usual course of training much milder forms of punishment are appropriate. It may be sufficient to work a little longer, to repeat an exercise, or perhaps to practise a difficult transition as a preparation for a movement that the horse has been evading.

The most effective punishments are those which are self inflicted. The horse who plunges his nose forwards to lengthen the reins or dislodge the rider will soon give up if his efforts merely result in pulling the rider down more firmly into the saddle. Horses that toss their heads

Photographic evidence is useful when analysing a horse's paces. Here we see a correct right lead canter. The left hind leg has landed and the legs of the left diagonal are stretching forward for the second beat of the stride. The horse is properly bent to the right, and he is straight. *(Photo: John Birt)*

about soon stop if the reins are held securely so that they bang their jaws against the bit.

Rewarding the horse when he has done well is a very important and oft neglected aspect of training. The best horses are those that look forward to their work and enjoy themselves. A happy horse will give a joyful, expressive performance. A gentle touch or a stroke on the neck is a good token of appreciation. A walk on a long rein is always very acceptable after strenuous exercise. The horse will always be ready to please if he thinks it will encourage his rider to dismount and take him back to the stable. Mints and sugar lumps can be very effective rewards too!

When schooling other people's horses safety is an important consideration. Before mounting it is prudent to find out if the horse is likely to be difficult or dangerous to ride, and to ask what his particular problems seem to be. It is also very important to maintain the highest standards and to try to uphold the fine tradition of classical riding. Correct methods must be demonstrated by example, and faulty approaches to schooling must be discouraged.

It is often necessary to offer advice on equipment. A jointed snaffle is usually the best bit to use, and any martingale should be removed unless the horse throws his head up to such an extent that the rider is liable to be hit in the face.

First of all it is essential to ensure that there is free forward movement and that the paces are correct. Secondly it is important to get the horse relaxed and rounded. Once that has been achieved it will be possible to evaluate and improve the balance, the straightness, and the rhythm. When the horse is moving correctly it will be appropriate to test the limits of collection and extension, and to investigate his capacity for lateral bending and lateral movement.

Educational deficiencies can usually be detected and remedied, but it should also be remembered that horses must be given the right signals if they are to respond correctly. It may be necessary to retrain their riders before any substantial or lasting progress can be made.

CHAPTER ELEVEN

Helpful Hints and Reminders

♦ The centuries old tradition of classical riding provides a systematic method of schooling the horse. Its object is to improve the horse physically and mentally, to make him pleasant and versatile to ride, and to prolong his useful working life. Regardless of what you do with your horse, if you train him this way you will be well pleased with the result. You do not have to take him all the way to advanced levels unless you want to specialise in high-school riding.

♦ Classical riding is one of the few branches of equestrianism that works with the horse's nature rather than against it. Accidents and injuries are rare. Casualties and sometimes even fatalities can be found in many of the other branches.

♦ Only if you aspire to do advanced work will you need to make a careful choice of horse. You can succeed up to medium level with almost any horse: conformation is not really critical at the lower levels.

♦ Understand the nature of the horse, and do not forget the lifestyle that nature intended him to have.

♦ Introduce the young horse gradually to human contact, equipment and training.

♦ Learn how to sit and how to move in harmony with the horse. Try to control him mainly through the seat. Learn to stop by using your thighs and abdominal muscles, and your back. Do not use the reins as a brake.

♦ Ensure that the horse carries your weight on his back and hind legs, rather than on his shoulders. Test your control of his back and his longitudinal stretching by practising lowering his neck at walk, trot and canter until the poll sinks down to the level of the withers.

♦ Check that you can still obtain the proper longitudinal flexion when you hold both reins in one hand. This will prove that you really are in control of the horse's back, and not merely influencing his neck by means of localised or unilateral rein effects.

♦ It is not natural for the horse to be above or behind the bit. If this happens then you or a previous rider must have caused the problem.

Check that you can lower the poll to the level of the withers.

♦ As the training progresses the horse should be capable of working in greater collection, which is to say he should be able to carry more weight on his haunches and lighten his shoulders. The pressure on the bit should diminish until it becomes negligible.

♦ The collected horse will work in a shorter frame, and you will be able to ride with shorter reins. The horse's natural head carriage defines the correct distance from the bit to your hands. Do not shorten the reins more than this, or you will put too much pressure on his jaw, and make his neck and your arms very tense.

♦ Collection cannot be achieved without active forward movement. When collection fails, try to develop the medium paces before making another attempt.

♦ Always be quick to deal with the major evasions of excessive speed, crookedness, and holding back instead of moving freely forwards.

♦ The straight horse has yet to be born: all horses are more or less one-sided. One of the objectives of schooling is to cure this problem. It is not necessary to call in the back specialist to manipulate the horse!

♦ Practising shoulder-in to the hollow side and quarters-in to the stiff side, and keeping the contact mainly on the rein of the hollow side, will prove particularly effective in alleviating one-sidedness.

♦ If you ride with both reins in one hand you may find it easier to detect crookedness, and you may find it easier to prevent the horse from evading your attempts at straightening him.

♦ It is perfectly acceptable to carry two schooling whips when training. You will not need to use them both at once, but it will mean you no longer have to keep moving the whip from side to side, and you will not miss the right moment for using it.

♦ Practise exercises for improving longitudinal and lateral flexion alternately.

♦ Two of the most effective training exercises are the half-halt and the shoulder-in.

♦ Impulsion is how easily you can ride the upward transitions. Balance is how easily you can ride the downward transitions.

♦ Except in the early stages of training, do not try to cover everything the horse can do in one lesson.

♦ Aim for perfection, but start to introduce new work when you are two thirds satisfied with the current work, otherwise you will stay forever at the same level.

♦ When results are elusive do not keep on attempting the same exercise. Try to discover the root cause of the problem, and be prepared to return to earlier work. Advanced work should fall into place easily. If it does not then there must be some problem with the foundation work upon which it depends.

♦ You cannot expect to improve the horse just by putting him through a set of selected exercises; knowledgeable application is also required. The horse is capable of cheating and evading everything you ask him to do, usually by increasing the tempo, or by going crookedly. You must be able to tell when the horse is not going correctly, and adjust the aids or change the exercise or pattern to try to coax him into a better way of going. Although you can plan the overall theme of a schooling session, you will have to ride the details according to the necessities of the moment.

♦ Nature can inspire the horse to perform most of the required movements within a few days of being born. You do not have to teach him anything he cannot do naturally. Your job is to learn how to direct his energies and to give him the freedom he needs to express himself as nature intended. Generally it is the rider himself who causes difficulties. When you have problems with an exercise, lengthen the reins and try again.

♦ Always try to discover the reason for resistances, and never provoke an argument that you cannot win. Always reward the horse when he does well. Remember that the voice can be a very useful aid.

♦ Every time you apply the aids try to make them a little lighter than last time. A higher level of refinement is always nearby waiting to be discovered.

♦ End every schooling session on a good note.

♦ If you can detect and correct imperfections quickly then you will make rapid progress. When you make mistakes try to learn from them. Training will get easier with experience.

Influential Riding Masters

Xenophon, a Greek statesman, General and horsemaster, lived from around 430 BC to 354 BC. He wrote the first completely surviving book on horsemanship, *Peri Hippikes*, in about 400 BC. This has appeared in modern translation as *The Art of Horsemanship*. Xenophon shows a great understanding of horse psychology, and clearly treated his animals kindly. He does not explain how young horses are to be trained, merely advising the rider to send his colts away to a horse-breaker. He describes how to sit, but gives little detail of schooling procedure. He used a jointed snaffle rather than a curb, and rode bareback.

Federico Grisone founded a riding academy in Naples in 1532. He rediscovered and adapted Xenophon's work, but lacked Xenophon's feel for the horse, and introduced more forceful methods. He wrote a book, *Gli Ordini di Cavalcare*, in 1550. Grisone described schooling exercises such as the volte and the serpentine. He employed the rein-back to get his horses more onto their haunches. Part of his manège was on an incline.

Count Césare Fiaschi was active in Naples at about the same time as Grisone. He published *A Treatise of Bridling, Schooling and Shoeing Horses* in 1556. He liked to school his horses to music, and was aware of the value of the voice as an aid.

Thomas Blunderville produced the first English books on riding. He published *The Art of Riding* around 1560 after being commissioned to translate Grisone. Grisone's ideas were also incorporated into *The Four Chiefest Offices of Horsemanship*, which he published in 1565.

Giambattista Pignatelli studied in Naples where he became Director of the riding academy. His methods were more humane than those of his teachers. He made use of pillars in his training. He used curbs, but recognised that the bit was not an item of major importance in training. By contemporary standards he worked with a relatively small selection of bits.

Salomon de la Broue lived from 1530 to 1610. He was a riding master at the court of the French King Henry IV. He studied in Naples under Pignatelli, but developed a better understanding of the nature of the horse, and was less forceful. In 1593 he published a book *Le Cavalerice François*. He pursued lightness and advocated a systematic training procedure, starting his horses with a cavesson, progressing to a snaffle, and finally working them in a curb.

Baron Georg Engelhard von Löhneysen, a Prussian, was born around 1550. He studied in Naples, and became the first German master of any consequence. He published *A Thorough Guide to Bridling and the Correct Use of Mouthpieces and Bits* in 1588, and *Della Cavalleria* in 1609.

Antoine Pluvinel de la Baume, 1555-1620, was riding master to Louis XIII of France. He studied under Pignatelli. Like Salomon de la Broue he adopted less forceful methods, and he treated his horses according to their individual needs. In 1593 he opened an academy in Paris. His book, *Maneige Royal*, was published posthumously in 1623. Before commencing mounted work, Pluvinel worked his horses in hand, lungeing them from a rope cavesson attached to a central pillar. He progressed very quickly to airs above the ground, which he taught between two pillars.

William Cavendish, Duke of Newcastle, lived from 1593 to 1676, and was undoubtedly the greatest English riding master of all time. A royalist, and tutor to the future Charles II, he opened a school in Antwerp whilst in exile during the Protectorate. He considered Grisone's methods outdated, but spoke highly of Pignatelli and

Pluvinel. He had an empathy with horses that is not always matched by modern trainers. He wrote *La Méthode Nouvelle et Invention Extroidinaire de Dresser Les Chevaux* in 1658, and another work, in English, *A New Method and Extraordinary Invention to Dress Horses*, in 1667. Newcastle gives advice on stud management and explains how colts should be broken for riding. He proceeds to present a detailed schooling programme which includes lateral work on the circle. By modern standards Newcastle worked very quickly, and was able to arrive at a level roughly comparable to our advanced medium dressage standard after a mere five months. He did not attempt airs above the ground, however, until much later. For this he used a single pillar, finding work between two pillars too restrictive. Newcastle recommended using the simplest bits available. He always started his horses with a cavesson before progressing to a bit, but he was quite capable of completing the training without using a bit.

François Robichon de la Guérinière was born in France around 1688 and died in 1751. He opened an academy in 1717, and in 1730 became master of Louis XIV's stables in the Tuileries, which had been founded by Pluvinel. In his book *École de Cavalerie*, published in 1729, he collected together all the best ideas of the earlier masters, paying tribute in particular to Salomon de la Broue and the Duke of Newcastle. La Guérinière made a major contribution by modifying the seat of the rider. Whereas the earlier masters had taught that the legs should be kept straight, he advised a more relaxed posture with a little bend in the knee. This allowed much gentler aiding and meant that it was possible to use shorter spurs. He also introduced the shoulder-in exercise on straight lines. La Guérinière's teaching is still valid today, and forms the basis of the training at the Spanish Riding School in Vienna.

Claude Bourgelat, 1712-1760, became Director of the Manège at Lyon. He rewrote Newcastle's work as *Le Nouveau Newcastle* in 1744. He was the first riding master to introduce three different types of trot.

Dom Pedro de Alcantara e Meneses, the 4th Marquis of Marialva, was born in 1713, and became Royal Master of the Horse to King José of Portugal. His civilised teaching methods were similar to those of La Guérinière and like the latter he pursued lightness.

Maximilian von Weyrother became Chief Rider of the Spanish Riding School in Vienna in 1825. He was responsible for establishing La Guérinière's teaching at the School. He published a book on bitting in 1814, and following his death in 1833 a further publication, *Fragments and Unpublished Writings*, appeared.

Louis Seeger, a German master born in 1794, studied under Weyrother. He published an important book *System der Reitkunst* in 1844, and died in 1865.

François Baucher, 1796-1873, was a French horsemaster of outstanding ability. His contribution to the art of classical riding was the introduction of one-time changes. His methods were not universally admired, partly because he thought of training in terms of overcoming resistances in the horse, and partly because he practised exercises such as the canter on the spot and the canter to the rear. Baucher published *Dictionnaire Raisonné d'Equitation* in 1833, and *Méthode d'Equitation basée sur le Nouveaux Principles* in 1842.

Count Antoine Cartier D'Aure was a French master who promoted the use of the rising trot and the working and extended paces. He lived from 1799 to 1863, and published a book, *Traite d'Equitation*, in 1834.

Gustav Steinbrecht became the most famous riding master of his day. He was born in Germany in 1808, and died in 1885. A pupil of Seeger, he trained horses for the circus, and published *Das Gymnasium des Pferdes* in 1885. An army manual based on his methods was published in 1912. It was Steinbrecht who coined the phrase: 'Ride your horse forward and straighten him'.

Baron Borries von Oeyenhausen, 1812-1875, became Chief Instructor at the Imperial Cavalry School of Salzburg in 1844. His book, *Guide to the Finishing of Horse and Rider*, published in 1848, is still in use today.

Field Marshal Franz Holbein von Holbeinsberg and **Chief Rider Johann Meixner** wrote their *Directives* for training at the Spanish Riding School in Vienna in 1898.

Bibliography

In writing this book I have been influenced by the following publications. They are listed in order of publication date.

Alois Podhajsky, *The Complete Training of Horse and Rider*, Harrap, London, 1967 (ISBN 0 245 59040 4).

Duke of Newcastle, *A General System of Horsemanship*, Winchester Press, New York, 1970 (ISBN 0 87691 022 3). This limited edition is a facsimile of a publication dating from 1753. It is not widely available.

General Decarpentry, *Academic Equitation*, J.A. Allen & Co. Ltd, London, 1971 (ISBN 0 85131 036 2).

Hans Handler, *The Spanish Riding School in Vienna*, Thames and Hudson Ltd, London, 1972 (ISBN 0 500 01092 7). This book is out of print, and is difficult to obtain.

Nuno Oliveira, *Reflections on Equestrian Art*, J.A. Allen & Co. Ltd, London, 1976 (ISBN 0 85131 250 0).

Charles de Kunffy, *Dressage Questions Answered*, published by Charles de Kunffy, Arizona, 1980 (ISBN 0 9601124 0 9).

Nuno Oliveira, *Notes and Reminiscences of a Portuguese Rider*, Howley and Russell, Caramut, Australia, 1982.

Nuno Oliveira, *Classical Principles of the Art of Training Horses*, Howley and Russell, Caramut, Australia, 1983 (ISBN 0 9591899 0 4).

Charles de Kunffy, *Creative Horsemanship*, Arco Publishing Inc., New York, 1984 (ISBN 0 668 05965 6).

Nuno Oliveira, *Horses and Their Riders*, Howley and Russell, Caramut, Australia, 1988 (ISBN 0 9591899 4 7).

Sylvia Loch, *The Classical Seat*, Unwin Hyman, London, 1988 (ISBN 0 04 440177 9).

Syliva Loch, *Dressage*, The Sportsman's Press, London, 1990 (ISBN 0 948253 46 0).

Hilda Nelson, *François Baucher: The Man and His Method*, J.A. Allen & Co. Ltd, London, 1992 (ISBN 0 85131 534 8).

♦ ♦ ♦

Below I have selected another ten books which I recommend for further study.

Alois Podhajsky, *The Art of Dressage*, Harrap, London, 1976 (ISBN 0 245 53027 4).

Richard L. Wätjen, *Dressage Riding*, J.A. Allen & Co. Ltd, London, 1979 (ISBN 0 85131 275 6).

Kathryn Denby-Wrightson and Joan Fry, *The Beginning Dressage Book*, Arco Publishing Inc., New York, 1981 (ISBN 0 668 04969 3).

Franz Mairinger, *Horses are Made to be Horses*, Rigby Publishers, Adelaide, Australia, 1983 (ISBN 0 7270 1795 0).

W. Müseler, *Riding Logic*, Methuen, London, 1983 (ISBN 0 413 53220 8).

Erik F. Herbermann, *The Dressage Formula*, J.A. Allen & Co. Ltd, London, 1984 (ISBN 0 85131 348 5).

German National Equestrian Federation, *The Principles of Riding*, Kenilworth Press, Bucks, 1985 (ISBN 1 872082 01 7).

German National Equestrian Federation, *Advanced Techniques of Riding*, Kenilworth Press, Bucks, 1986 (ISBN 1 872082 33 5).

Brigadier General Kurt Albrecht, *A Dressage Judge's Handbook*, J.A. Allen & Co. Ltd, London, 1988 (ISBN 0 85131 459 7).

Charles de Kunffy, *The Athletic Development of the Dressage Horse*, Macmillan Publishing Co., New York and London, 1992 (ISBN 0 87605 896 9).

Index

Page numbers in *italics* refer to illustrations.

Aids 24–6, 32–9, 57, 71–8
Arms 21–3

Backing the horse 103–4
Balance 51–5, 114, 118
Baucher, François 79, 123
Bending 71–4
Bit 101
   above the 32–7, 116
   behind the 32–5, 116
   curb 38
   on the 32
Blunderville, Thomas 120–1
Boots 100
Bourgelat, Claude 122
Bridle, double 30, 109

Canter 24, 46, 103–7, *113*
   counter- 47, 108, 110
   pirouette 93–8
Cavendish, William *see*
   Newcastle, Duke of
Cavesson, lungeing 100
Collection 23, 55, 85–98, 105, 117
Contact 21–3, 46
Control, principles of 24–6
Counter
   canter 47, 108
   change of hand 110
   flexion 48–9

Crookedness 39–50 *see also*
   One-sidedness
Curb bit 38

D'Aure, Antoine Cartier 123
de Kunffy, Charles 9, 11
de la Broue, Salomon 121

Equitation 18–24

Fear 57
Fiaschi, Césare 120
Flexion 38, 48, 117
Flying changes 79–84, 108, 110
Forehand, turn on the 60–1
Forward movement 27–31, 114
Full pass 67, 107

Ganimedes 97
Gigolo 25
Grisone, Federico 120

Half-halt 26, 37, 54, 118
Half-pass 43, 49, 66, 77–8, 107
   canter *94*–5, 109
Halt 106–7
Haunches-in 43–4, 48, 64–7, 75–6, 107, 110
Haunches-out 64–7, *95*, 110
Haunches, turn on the *69*, 108
Head carriage 32

Hill work 54

Impulsion 29, 118
In-hand work 106, 109
Interference by rider 29–30

Jumping 106

Klimke, Reiner *40*
Kottas, Arthur *19, 53*

La Guérinière, François de 62, 79, 122
Lateral movements 48–50, 54, 59–70, 74–8
Laziness 30–1, 57
Legs 20–1
Leg-yield 61–3
Loins 54–5
Lungeing 101–4

Martingale 114
Meixner, Johann 123
Movement, forward 27–31, 114

Newcastle, Duke of 62, 121–2

Oliveira, Nuno 86
Olympic Cocktail 65
One-sidedness 27, 41, 117 *see also*
    Crookedness

Pain 57
Passade 67–8, 110
Passage 91–3, 110
Pedro de Alcantara e Meneses 122–3
Pelvis 24, 55
Physiological problems 31
Piaffe 85, 86–91, 109–10
Pignatelli, Giambattista 121
Pirouette 68–70, 85, 93–8, 110
Pluvinel de la Baume, Antoine 121
Punishment 112–14

Quarters falling in 46–7

Rein-back 106, 108
Rein contact 46
Reins 21–3, 37–9

draw *33*, 38
running 38
side 102–3
Rembrandt 90
Resistances 56–8, 118–19
Reward 114
Rider interference 29–30
Roller 100

Safety 114
Schooling 106–14, *see also* Training
Seat 18–20
Seeger, Louis 123
Shoulder-in 43–4, 48, 62–4, 74–5
    in schooling 107, 117–18
Shoulder-fore 48–9
Snaffle 101, 114
Spanish Riding School 79, 86, *102*, 122–3
Speed 29–30
Spurs 31, 107
Steinbrecht, Gustav 123
Stopping 24–6, *see also* Half-halt
Straightening the horse 39–50
Stride, lengthening and
    shortening 54, 89, 103

Theodorescu, Monica *97*
'Tornado' 95
Training procedure 99–110
Transitions 26, 52, 54, 105–8, 110, 118
Trot 23, *25*, 89, 103–5

Uphoff, Nicole *90*

Van Grunsven, Anky *65*
Von Holbeinsberg, Franz 123
Von Lühneysen, Georg Engelhard 121
Von Oeyenhausen, Borries 123
Von Weyrother, Maximilian 123

Walk 23, 104–5, 108
Werth, Isabell *25*
Whip 117

Xenophon 120

Young horses 34–5, 111–2, 115